# THE LEARNING ZONE

## MAXIMISE YOUR POTENTIAL

# The Learning Zone

## maximise your potential

Felicity Heathcote

*Psychologist to the Irish Olympic Team*
*Sydney 2000*

WOLFHOUND PRESS

Published in 2000 by
Wolfhound Press Ltd
68 Mountjoy Square
Dublin 1, Ireland
Tel: (353-1) 874 0354
Fax: (353-1) 872 0207



British Library Cataloguing in Publication Data
A catalogue record for this book is available from the British Library.

ISBN 0-86327-798-5

10 9 8 7 6 5 4 3 2 1



*The Essential Haiku: Versions of Bashō, Buson and Issa,* Edited by Robert Hass, © 1994 Ecco Press
'Alone' by Clare Holohan from *The Whole Shebang,* © 1998 The O'Brien Press
*Hafiz: Fifty Poems*, A.J. Arberry, ©1974 Cambridge University Press
*Dewdrops on a Lotus Leaf: Zen Poems of Ryokan,* John Stevens (trans.), © 1993 Shambhala Centaur Editions
*The Rubáiyát of Omar Khayyám*, Edward Fitzgerald (trans.), © 1993 Wordsworth Editions Limted
*Wisdom Keepers,* Arden, Harvey and Wall, Steve (eds), © 1990 Beyond Words Publishing

For permission to reproduce extracts of this material we gratefully acknowledge the above.

Front cover photograph: Slide File
Cover Design: Wolfhound Press
Typesetting and book design: Wolfhound Press
Printed in the Republic of Ireland by ColourBooks, Dublin

# Acknowledgements

My thanks to Niall, Clare and Andrew, whose patience and support have been unending.

My thanks are also due to the following:

To members of the Olympic Council of Ireland – especially President Pat Hickey, Vice-President Dermot Sherlock, Barry Holohan, Martin Burke, Peadar Casey, Dr Joseph Cumisky, Dr Marie-Elaine Grant, Catherine Murray, and special thanks to Willie O'Brien, Billy Kennedy and Tom Rafter who organised the OCI educational workshops for Olympic Athletes 2000.

To Janet Spears, the Principal of Public School 97; Staff Developer Mary Spellman, and all of the staff and students of that school – a place that celebrates excellence. Also to the memory of Richard Pochter, a very special teacher.

To Irene H. Impellizzeri, Vice-President of the New York Education Board, for her interest in these ideas.

To the staff and students of St Joseph's School, Bronxville, New York, especially Patricia McAdam, Ginny Deckelmann, and Tim Chapman.

To Dr Hiro Ueki, Eliza Kimball, Colonel Maurice Canavan, John Frier, and Mark Tran at the United Nations, New York.

To the Royal Irish Academy of Music, Dublin – students and staff and in particular Dr John O'Conor, Dorothy McCauley, Aisling McCormack and Therese Murphy.

To colleagues and friends in different countries who have exchanged ideas and offered me much encouragement: William Johnston SJ, Yoshiko Ushioda, Jim Mullen, Nell Lauber, Fr Brendan Duggan, Kitty St Onge, Carole Walsh, Mick Desmond, Ciaran Fitzpatrick, Brenda Biggar, Linda Castro, Margot Bohl, Carol Pugh, Margaret Leahy, Liam Brophy, Judy Woodworth, John Lalor, Renagh Holohan, Mary Patterson, Madeleine Tunney, Michelle Faulkner, Áine Conlon, Aidan O'Beirne, Phil O'Dowd, Donal Mc Auliff, Maggie Klee Lichtenberg, Leslie Lalor, Ann O'Reilly, Gai Griffin, David and Richard Watchorn, Pat Block, Penny Carroll, Michael Dillon, Máire O'Carroll, Teresa Tully, Eleanor Heathcote, Peter Keating, David Cassidy, Eithne Barry, Sonja Tiernan, Imelda McCarthy, Dr Joan Artus.

To André and Colm of Darius Design, whose ideas and work have been invaluable to me over the years. Also to my friends who have spent much time and thought in the preparation of this book – Catherine McDonnell, Elizabeth Fuller, Rosemary Haugh and Evelyn Devereux.

To all of the students who have used these techniques and shared their ideas with me, including: Michael, Eoin, Eike, Ronan, Una, Gerard, Stephanie, Andrea, Eamon, Orla, Dominic, Sanam, Claire, Catherine, Frances, Sarah, William, Vivienne, Laura, Stephen, Ciara, Moira, James and Kate.

To my publisher, Seamus Cashman, and everyone at Wolfhound Press especially Emer Ryan and Jennifer Treacy for their patience and hard work, and my editor, David Houlden, whose good humour made a difficult task seem so much easier.

# Contents

To the memory of my parents

to my father whose love of learning
taught me to search for knowledge
both in books and in life
and
to my mother whose loving sense of calm
allowed me to be myself

# FOREWORD

> All is quiet at the still point of the turning world.
>
> WILLIAM JOHNSTON

Over the years working with students and professionals in Trinity College, I have come to realise that concentration is of paramount importance. Successful performances in all areas of life require relaxed concentration, yet few books or educationalists have ever explored this area in any great detail.

Without the ability to focus single-mindedly on what they are doing, even the most talented student, athlete or artist is unable to achieve success consistently. When the human mind is disturbed by thoughts of success or failure, concentration is broken, anxiety is increased and the performance of the individual deteriorates – clarity of thought is clouded and lost. A thousand years ago, it was suggested by Zen monks that our minds are thrown into confusion if we allow ourselves to be distracted by thoughts of greed and glory. In today's hectic society, the same still holds true – from the classroom to the boardroom and beyond. In particular, the inability to concentrate can be a major factor in the lack of achievement frequently experienced by students of all ages on the academic treadmill.

The purpose of this book is to help students, or other creative individuals, to fulfil their potential – to perform as well as they can at any given time – by achieving a state of relaxed concentration. This mental state of heightened awareness – called by many the 'zone' or 'flow state' – is necessary for peak performance in all areas of study preparation, exam taking and artistic performance.

Over the last two decades, Felicity Heathcote has used an adapted form of Zen meditation to help individuals to achieve a state of optimal functioning of body and mind. This 'Peak Performance' programme was devised and put into practice for the Irish Olympic team and proved particularly successful at the 1992 Barcelona games. It was found that the positive results experienced by the athletes in this highly competitive environment were capable of being extended to all aspects of their lives. As a result, the programme has been successfully modified for use with students of all ages and with those engaged in all types of creative pursuits.

Students, and others, have discovered that a distractionless state of mind is achievable when they meditate correctly; when they enter the right state of mind, their minds are quite clear and flowing. As a music student remarked, he reached a state of '... nothing but pure clarity and great focus in an otherwise cluttered mind'.

Likewise, when applied to a class of primary school children in a public school in the New York borough of the Bronx, it was found that the programme achieved a remarkable response from both pupils and teachers alike. Measurable results were outstanding. Indeed, many of the students involved in the programme in the Bronx, and elsewhere, used the techniques they had learnt for other aspects of their career preparation – including interviews. Over the years, in my own work, I have found poor concentration to be a major problem for many students. Consequently, I have recommended this programme to many second- and third-level students. The improvement in their level of concentration has been remarkable.

Those who read this book and put its principles into practice should be capable of similar results. It is intended for all who wish to achieve more from whatever they are doing but particularly for those students at school or at college who feel that their full potential is not being realised and who are capable of a great deal more than they are achieving at present.

ERIC GUIRY BA, BD, LIC PHIL, DCG, H DIP ED, MA
CAREERS ADVISER
TRINITY COLLEGE DUBLIN

# INTRODUCTION

Lost! One golden Hour
Set with Sixty Diamond minutes.
No Reward is Offered
For It Is GONE FOR EVER!

KATHERINE MANSFIELD

The bright lights flickered and glowed along the darkened Mediterranean coast as we flew high above. For me that night, the lights reflected the hopes and dreams of the athletes returning to Dublin after the Barcelona Olympic Games. Some of the athletes on that plane had fulfilled their potential and dreams, others had not – it was this that would always matter more than medals. I had worked for many years helping Olympic athletes to utilise their talents and skills to the full. Now, however, that chapter had come to a close and I wondered how the next one would unfold. My husband, Niall, had just been posted to the United Nations in New York for five years and I was about to join him there (previously I had been with him on postings to Tokyo and Tehran).

While resident in New York, I had written my book *Peak Performance: Zen and the Sporting Zone* (Wolfhound Press, 1996), in which I explain my techniques of taking the principles of Zen and applying them to the training of athletes. Shortly after publication of this book, I was asked by one of the teachers of PS (Public School) 97, in the Bronx, to give a talk to the children about my work. I then had the idea to see how my concentration techniques could be adapted to help the children of this school improve their performance in study and exams*. I had done this kind of work previously, in Ireland, with older students and I was very interested to avail of this new opportunity to work with children who were both younger and from a completely different background and culture.

Around this time I had begun, in my mind, to write a second book – a more general one – on how Zen techniques can influence and improve all areas of our lives. From the start, however, my pen took on a life of its own and began to write a different book from that which I had first conceived – it was a book with its emphasis on study and creativity. Just as, over the centuries, the Japanese masters of *Kyudo* (archery) had talked of 'it shot' rather than 'I shot', so too my pen began to write of its own accord. I contacted my publisher, Seamus Cashman, to explain that the nature of my second book had now changed. This book is the result of my pen's flight.

* Some of the schoolchildren's comments on the techniques appear throughout the book. These quotations are reproduced as they were originally written, including spelling and grammar.

The Learning Zone is intended for those of all ages who are in the education system – teachers and students alike – for musicians and painters and writers; indeed, for anyone who is attempting to do something better than they have ever done it before, and also to do it in a more creative fashion. I hope that children and students of all subjects will use these ideas to reach for the stars and, as a result, spend their lives on the path to 'perfection of action'. The more general book I had intended to write will have to wait for another day.

FELICITY HEATHCOTE
PSYCHOLOGIST TO THE IRISH OLYMPIC TEAM
SYDNEY 2000

# Part I

## Zen and the Way to Peak Performance

Before the performance in the concert hall I sat for a few minutes at a time – breathing. Walking on to the stage, I felt great. I enjoyed the singing and was very happy with it.

STUDENT, ROYAL IRISH ACADEMY OF MUSIC, DUBLIN

# CHAPTER 1

## The Road to Perfection

We all have within us a centre of stillness.

DAG HAMMARSKJÖLD
(UNITED NATIONS SECRETARY GENERAL, 1953–1961)

### Focused Energy

For many of us, as we reach the beginning of the twenty-first century, we seem to be spinning in never-ending circles, our restless minds out of control. As we search for a sense of fulfilment in our noisy, space-age world, maybe it is time to look at our lives and rediscover that it is in the centre of stillness, referred to many times by Dag Hammarskjöld, that we find perfection and a sense of calm. In this area of quietude of the soul we find the ability to develop and use our talents to the full – to achieve excellence in whatever we do. In fact, there is reason to believe that the achievement of our own peak performance – whether in athletics, art or in any other form of human activity – appears only to be reached while we are in touch with this centre. As we lose ourselves in our actions, we seem to experience changes in time and in spatial dimensions. We may feel as if we are being guided in our speech or actions or that our pen is writing on its own as our minds work with great clarity, effortlessly retrieving the information for that important exam; our minds like mirrors, reflecting unnecessary distractions. In essence, what this really means is that our energy is focused on the task in hand in order that we can achieve our own personal excellence.

## Timeless Flow*

Several decades ago, I became aware that a state of relaxed concentration can be achieved, by use of a specific technique, when I started to work with the Irish Olympic team. I realised that this state of the 'zone' or 'timeless flow' was a perfect state of clarity of thought and action. In this focused mental state, the individual was aware of all internal and external stimuli but only tuned into what was relevant, everything flowed without effort and temporal or spatial dimensions were sometimes altered. Thus a musician would be aware of the audience but not be affected by it; the schoolchild undertaking an exam might hear extraneous noises but would pay no attention to them; the athlete likewise can focus completely on the task in hand aware of, but not distracted by, the other competitors. If, however, the athlete has to attend to certain conditions, such as the wind direction, then he would be aware of this and make the appropriate adjustments.

* The concept of 'flow' has been developed by Mihaly Csikszentmihalyi – see *The Evolving Self* (HarperCollins, 1993) and *Flow: The Psychology of Optimal Experience* (Harper and Row, 1990)

## 'An Angel Held Me'

For many years it was not thought possible to tune into this state of mind of one's own volition. It was believed to occur either naturally or not at all. By means of adapting a form of Christian Zen meditation, which I had studied during the years when I lived in Japan, however, I devised a 'Peak Performance' programme (outlined in Chapter 6) whereby it became possible for athletes and others to harness this seemingly elusive state of mind.

In this special 'Peak Performance' state one young American girl remarked that, when skating, she felt: '... as if everything flowed; when the music ended I felt as if an angel held me and made me do all the moves – perfectly.' This eleven-year-old was describing the 'zone' or 'flow state' which is often identified by top world athletes as 'magic'. Magical it may be, but it is, in fact, a time of quiet satisfaction, of peace and focused energy – not one of arrogance and self-obsession. This state is probably most clearly experienced in sporting excellence but it is, of course, also achievable in all aspects of life. Although it is possible for us all to attain this unique state of mind, it occurs infrequently – even for top performers at world level. Over the last twenty years, I have found that an adapted Zen meditation programme appears to be the most effective way to tune into this quiet state of mind, this centre of stillness.

## Room of Quiet

Nearly four decades ago, Dag Hammarskjöld appears to have been aware of the importance of meditation. In the foyer of the United Nations building, overlooking the fast-flowing East

River in the busy city of New York, is a meditation room. It is situated beside the jewel-coloured stained-glass window designed by Marc Chagall, and a glass case containing a piece of rock from the moon. Dag Hammarskjöld set up this 'room of quiet' for UN diplomats, and he himself visited it just before his fateful journey to find a solution to the problems in Katanga, where he died in a plane crash in 1961. This room is now kept locked, but is opened, at the request of delegates, to allow individuals and groups to be there alone with their thoughts in the darkened peace. A large mural, by Swedish artist Bo Boskow, covers the end wall, and a slab of black iron-ore sits starkly alone in the centre of the small room; the lighting arrangement throws out an oblong glow of light on the floor reflecting the shape of the iron-ore 'altar'. An inscription at the entrance guides the visitor with the words: 'A room of quiet where only thoughts should speak.'

## World Stage

In his book *Markings*, Dag Hammarskjöld at times writes more like an Eastern sage or Christian mystic than an international bureaucrat. He realised, long before meditation became popular in the West, how necessary it was for everyone – especially those involved in the search for world peace – to achieve an uncluttered, unbiased mental state. He was aware of how difficult it was in our over-stimulated age to tune in to this state of mind – free of distractions, free of egotism. He knew only too well the perils of self-interest on the world stage, how the desire for fame and glory could easily supersede the important rôle of carrying out a good job. In order to truly succeed, it is necessary to forget the self, and to concentrate fully on the task in hand. As Hammarskjöld himself pointed out: 'To reach perfection, we must all pass one by one, through the death of self-effacement.'[1]

## Zen Practice

I often touched this 'centre of stillness' in Tokyo, a city full of noise and crowded with people, when lecturing at Sophia University many years ago. It was at this Jesuit university that many famous professors initiated dialogue between Christianity and Buddhism in the 1960s and 1970s. It was here too that the American Trappist monk, Thomas Merton, was to hold discussions with Sophia academics after his meeting with the Dalai Lama in 1968. I began to study Christian Zen with well-known professors, William Johnston and Kadawaki, in the mid 1970s. I tried to live more truly from day to day, really seeing the beauty of the world around me; wondering at the tiny flower lost in the crack in the wall, the ancient wooden temple half-hidden by the overpowering skyscrapers. Ironically, the significance of these things was enhanced, rather than diminished, by their relative lack of size and apparent unimportance. To see – to really see, not just to look – is a far more developed art in the Orient than in the West; there is indeed much that we can learn from the study of Eastern thought processes.

> The less we see, the more numbed we become to the joy and pain of being alive...
>
> FREDERICK FRANCK[2]

To go through life in harmony with ourselves, with others and with our surroundings – to live a full and vital life – is perhaps one of the most important lessons we can learn. I have read a lot about Zen and have compared it with great interest to many old teachings and religions. I have been inspired by much of this reading, but it has been my own experience, my putting Christian Zen into practice in my life and work over two decades, that has taught me most of all.

## Perfection of Mind

> In training, you must test and polish yourself in order to face the great challenges of life.
>
> MORIHEI UESHIBA[3]

Back in Ireland, working with the Irish Olympic team in the late 1970s, I realised that the state of mind attained in Zen meditation was similar to the 'zone' – or 'flow state' – in which the athletes achieve their best performance. Little was known about this subject at the time. There was even a fear of talking about this mental state because the experience was often so intense and the effects sometimes so unusual that athletes thought they might be regarded as crazy. At that time it was believed that it was not possible to induce this state; in fact, as athletes acknowledged, as soon as its presence was recognised, it was gone. As a result, trying to persuade individuals that it might be possible to induce and control this state at will has not been an easy task over the last two decades. Recently, however, there has been much interest in the 'zone', and scientific studies now suggest it may indeed be a 'meditative state'. In the 'zone' there are temporal and spatial changes; distractions are not attended to, and the athletes find themselves in a cocoon of supreme concentration in which necessary stimuli are attended to and distractions are let go. Twenty years ago, I worked out a programme of Zen meditation which I felt might help the athletes to harness this perfect state of mind. The results were excellent; the first Olympic athlete that I dealt with talked excitedly, not about his improved scores (in archery), but about the fact that he had learnt to attain 'perfection of mind'. Ironically, the less affected he was by his scores the more they improved. He learnt that by letting go of the need to win, his performance actually improved and he achieved 'an aimless aim'. Years later, I travelled to Barcelona as the official psychologist to the Irish Olympic team. By this time, I had tried out these techniques extensively and had achieved equally good results with both individual and team sports, as well as in other areas in life.

## Sea of Pebbles

Calligraphy of geese
against the sky –
the moon seals it

BUSON[4]

Zen thought has been used as a basis for the martial arts and many other aspects of Japanese culture over several centuries. When I was living in Japan, I was fascinated by the simplicity of *Haiku* poetry, the beauty of the Japanese black-and-white ink painting, the old wooden architecture that had so inspired Frank Lloyd Wright, and the Zen gardens – rocks rising out of a sea of pebbles. The essential thread linking all aspects of Japanese culture is composure of mind. Yoshiko Ushioda[5], who was the Japanese Curator of the Chester Beatty Library in Dublin, pointed out: 'No matter how excellent or talented one may be, a peaceful state of mind is an essential element for true success.' Ushioda *Sensei* (teacher) felt that a calm, composed state of mind – a state of mental perfection – is necessary not only for sport but for all activities and performances in life. Over the last two decades, I have used Zen meditation to help myself and others to tune into this state of mind for art, writing, business, exams, health and many other aspects of life.

## Lifeless Lectures

I started to get particularly interested in the application of my theories to education when I was approached by a friend of mine, Hilda O'Connell, ten years ago. Hilda, a social worker in Dublin, asked me whether these ideas could help students with their exam anxiety. At this stage, I began to work out a programme for high school and college levels in which the student could approach exams and study in the same way as an athlete would treat a competition or a sports practice session. I began to realise that sport encompasses the emotions and ambitions of the whole of life – the problems, the successes, the pride, shame, joy, sadness, boredom and exhilaration. It exposes individuals to great stress and forces them to devise coping methods while, at the same time, allowing them to push forward the boundaries of their own personal excellence.

Over the years, I became fascinated by what constituted a good lecture, having sat through many a lifeless talk from professors who were more interested in their own ego or research, than in the progress of their students. I have also attended many wonderful and inspiring lectures which made me want to go out and search for more information on the given subject. What was the difference? The main difference seemed to be that the lecturers in the latter category spoke with passion about their subject and were interested in their students or their listeners; they spoke from the heart, not trying to impress, not distracted by the reaction of their audience. In the end, there was only a silence – a stillness that touched our souls as we were drawn into the various worlds of the lecturers and we became part of each one's state of perfection.

## Love of Subject

I taught in universities and gave public lectures in many different countries, constantly working on how to become a better lecturer. Ironically, it was only when I forgot to try hard, when I began to concentrate on the love of my subject and the development of ideas, that my lecturing began to improve. As I let go, I became more 'Zen-like' in my own approach and less interested in making an impression on others; I relied on my intuition to tell me whether or not I was performing well. We don't need to ask for affirmation from others for our actions – we know only too well how we are doing if we listen to our own intuition.

Teaching students to improve their study and exam technique, and helping teachers to teach more efficiently, are really two sides of the same coin. Preparing handouts for children's lessons and teachers' workshops very soon taught me that! Learning to be an excellent teacher, and a well-rounded, successful student, are approaches that, up to recently, have to a large part been ignored. Both rôles involve organisational techniques, motivation, and an ability to produce a state of relaxed concentration (the 'flow state' or 'zone'). To teach time management skills and organisational ability is important but to induce a state of motivation and flow is a more complex matter. The carrot and stick policy of rewards and punishment has long been developed and used in behavioural psychology, but to rely on long-term improvement by these methods may not be so useful. In many different parts of the world, teachers are becoming much more stressed and ineffectual, while students, for their part, are becoming prone to play truant and to underachieve. It may now be preferable to approach education in a different and more creative way.

## Self-seeking

Wealth and place breed insolence
That brings ruin in its train

LAO TZU[6]

Over two thousand years ago, the Chinese Taoist sages wrote about the dangers of the excesses of their time. Their writings could be said to have particular relevance to the final decades of the twentieth century. This very materialistic period, which continues at the outset of the new century, sees a lack of balance in the lives of many individuals. It is a time of self-seeking and self-obsession, when power politics play a major rôle, especially in business. People, ethics, and the concept of job performance being undertaken to the best of one's ability, seem, for many, to be of little relevance. Everyone needs to win – by fair means or foul – and as we all know there are very few outright winners in life; as a result, many talented individuals are often pushed aside or simply decide to opt out of the race altogether. Getting to the top, however, often does not prove to be as rewarding or exciting as is thought. For many it is a short-lived and disappointing experience.

Maybe in the twenty-first century we can view the game of life differently; perhaps we can all be winners after all! Instead of concentrating on having to be the best, on beating others into the ground and grabbing everything for ourselves, perhaps society's thinking can be changed so that being the very best we can be becomes the goal for everyone. If we do this, we will all have won because we can do no more and a feeling of true fulfilment will become one of our rewards; this sense of satisfaction means that we can also delight in the joy of others. This inner knowledge of our own success is one of the most important things that we can achieve, although, unfortunately, we don't always realise this.

One of the top Paralympic athletes, Patrice Dockery, did understand this very clearly. She told me how she threw aside her medal with disgust after one competition, because she realised that she had achieved a better time in training the previous week. She knew that others thought her medal was a wonderful achievement but she realised it wasn't as special as they believed because, in fact, she had under-performed. On another occasion, although she didn't win a medal, Patrice was really delighted when she achieved her best times and performance. As in other aspects of life, we know only too well when we have done our very best – that is when we are in the 'zone' – and only then do we feel truly satisfied with our performance.

## Objective Measures

> When in the 'zone' I feel like a magnet and the ball is like a piece of metal.
>
> TONY O'DOWD[7]
> ST PATRICK'S ATHLETIC FOOTBALL CLUB

A few years ago, some American sports psychologists suggested that the concept of doing our best was too vague and thus unlikely to produce concrete results. I found, however, that putting emphasis on a goal, such as obtaining medals or achieving improved times or scores, causes pressure and, as a result, the performance often deteriorates. It is my opinion that there is a more objective measure of doing our best – that is whether or not the individual is in the 'zone'. When I have asked individuals about times when they have achieved their 'peak performance', they all acknowledged that, like Patrice, they had been in the 'flow state'. On other occasions, even if they had won a medal, they were not happy with their performance unless they had achieved a perfect state of mind. Only in the 'flow state' do I myself find that I can give my best talks or do my best work – aware of the audience but not attending to them, solving problems and answering questions easily and without hesitation.

## Exam Technique

> Whatever they may paint of nature will inevitably be expressive of this intuition; the 'spirit of the mountains' will be felt softly breathing in their works.
>
> D.T. SUZUKI[8]

Over the years, I began using the meditation programme that I had devised, with high school and college students. The athletes among them often used the meditation to improve both their sporting ability and their exam techniques. If this is the state of mind in which the athlete can perform to the peak of his or her ability, then it is also the state where excellence can be achieved in both academic and creative subjects. In fact, this appears to be the mental state in which we fulfil our potential and do our best work in whatever we do. Many people find it distressing that they have achieved the 'zone' or 'flow state' infrequently or not at all, in any intense, memorable way. This is not a reason to get upset, but rather one to help us to realise that so much more can be attained. In previous years, it wasn't believed possible to achieve this state at will, rather it was seen to be a 'hit or miss' affair. One top US athlete, who was lecturing with me at a seminar in University College Dublin several years ago, told me that although he was the holder of a silver Olympic medal and a world championship title, he was still unable to enter this state of relaxed concentration of his own volition. Had he been able to do so, how many more medals might he have won over the years?

## Academic Setting

> First, before putting the feather on your nose, you have to forget everything – just put the feather on your nose, don't get distracted! Even if somebody said the President is in this room, don't listen, concentrate on the feather!
>
> ELEVEN-YEAR-OLD STUDENT, PUBLIC SCHOOL 97
> THE BRONX, NEW YORK

Initially I wasn't sure whether the 'zone' could play a significant rôle in the training of younger children. Although they can naturally lose themselves in creative play more easily and much more often than older individuals, I was still unsure if this state could be utilised by them in a more formal academic or creative setting. In fact, even the simple concept of concentration does not yet seem to play any significant rôle in most schools, or even colleges of higher education, in Europe or the United States. During my stay in New York, I was asked by a teacher, Mary Spellman, to give a talk to a public school in the Bronx (PS 97).

There were also to be other speakers at the occasion on which I was invited to deliver my talk who, as it turned out, all happened to have been past pupils of the school. (These included Dr Eric Rose, who had been on the medical team that had carried out the heart transplant on the brother of Yankee's manager Joe Torres days before the Yankees won the World Series in 1996.)

The reason I had been invited to talk was that I had just recently written a book about sport (the school is a 'school for writers' associated with the Columbia University writing programme). I felt, however, that my talk would be more relevant if I first went to the school, met the children and discussed my ideas with them. This, I thought, was necessary as I came from a completely different country and culture. Despite the fact that many of the children came from socially disadvantaged backgrounds, it was a very impressive school and everyone there seemed to be open to the new ideas. With this in mind, I began by doing sessions with several classes from the fourth and fifth grades – comprising nine- to eleven-year-olds – teaching them to focus their energy and combining my ideas with various reading and writing strategies used by Mary Spellman and the other teachers.

The teachers and teaching methods in the school were excellent, and all greatly contributed to the work I was doing. A positive, focused mental state will obviously not, of itself, produce brilliant results without good teaching and hard work. Most teachers, however, would admit that the main problem for many children is an inability to focus. Mary, in her rôle as reading teacher in the New York school system, taught the children many excellent reading and testing strategies. She acknowledged, however, that: 'Something was lacking because many children couldn't even stay focused long enough to complete their reading tests.'

It seemed likely that the millions of dollars flowing into New York schools every year, which were to be used on impressive new methods and facilities, were in fact not being utilised as adequately as they might have been. One of the main reasons for this was that many of the children were unable to concentrate sufficiently in order to take advantage of the new ideas and techniques.

## Self-esteem

> Well, it relaxs you and takes all your worries. It makes you feel a lot better than before. It clears your mind, and puts you straight into concentration.
>
> TEN-YEAR-OLD STUDENT, PUBLIC SCHOOL 97
> THE BRONX, NEW YORK

My initial work with Public School 97 was the beginning of one of the most rewarding and exciting projects of my life. It was fascinating to see the enthusiasm of the young children as they began to feel more in control, and learnt that they were beginning to be the best they could be. Their self-esteem appeared to increase naturally because they were feeling better about themselves. They also recognised that they were capable of achieving more than they had in the past. Instead of being fed empty affirmations when – deep down – they didn't feel too good about themselves, they began to realise that what they had achieved was special even if they weren't top of the class. As one young boy, Michael – whose marks had increased substantially from the previous year – remarked: 'I am really happy with my marks in the New York State test, even if I didn't get on the ninetieth percentile. I did my breathing and my reading strategies, and I did my very best. My parents are very happy, and they gave me a present.' Michael wasn't upset that he wasn't the best in the class, he was aware that, at that particular time, he had done his very best and that his score had improved. He no longer worried about comparing himself with others.

## Spirituality

Over the years, most aspects of spirituality have been cut out of public school life in New York. Probably, as the city is a place of such diverse cultures, beliefs and creeds, it was initially done for a good reason.

However, like all good ideas, many people feel that this has now been taken to extremes. The children, nevertheless, bring their own spirituality to their lives and I believe that this will all eventually come full circle. It is quite difficult for me to discuss my ideas while avoiding the mention of any philosophical or spiritual concepts.

Generally speaking, however, I did manage to do so, but I was very definitely put in my place by a young child on one particular occasion. The children were in the playground discussing the similarities between the 'zone' and a film (*Angels in the Outfield*) in which a child was the only one who could see an angel helping various members of a baseball team to perform superbly. 'You don't have to think of an angel standing behind you,' I said hastily. The nine-year-old child stood in front of me defiantly: 'I believe in angels,' she said, 'I've seen an angel!' So much for attempting to cut spirituality out of the curriculum!

This brings to mind a piece of native American wisdom which suggests the idea that when we see the wonders of nature:

> ... the sun, the moon, and the stars in the sky, anyone must realise that it is the work of someone more powerful than man.
>
> CHASED-BY-BEARS (1843–1915)
>
> SANTEE-YANKTONAI SIOUX[9]

## Acceptance of Concepts

I simplified the ideas behind the 'Peak Performance' programme quite considerably to make them more easily understandable to young children. We didn't talk about meditation as such; we talked about breathing. We didn't do the breathing for very long, just two or three breaths, and we didn't go into any philosophy; we simply attempted to achieve our best and to see activity as a joyful challenge. To my delight, the children rapidly accepted the concepts with great enthusiasm.

Of course, the fact that they were involved in a version of a programme used previously by world athletes was helpful. Mary and the other teachers worked very well with me, which was most important, as I could not go to the school very often. The reaction of the children confirmed my belief that the psychological side of any aspect of life is like a piece of a jigsaw puzzle; it may be only a minor part but if the piece is missing then the puzzle cannot be completed. The children took the programme far beyond the stage that I believed was possible at that age. They themselves modified and used the ideas in other situations. One nine-year-old, Laura, had been assigned to help a friend with her maths problems: 'We do our breathing together,' she told me proudly, 'and then we do our math, it really helps.' Another child had written a story about a friend who was in an abusive family: 'I wish I had known about these techniques last year,' she said, 'perhaps I could have helped my friend's family.'

Other children used the techniques for visits to the doctor or when having blood samples taken or for coping with noisy siblings in cramped home conditions. Maybe we underestimate the ingenuity and creativity of young children – certainly the results of our project would suggest that.

## Clearing Doubts and Panic

At this stage, the programme was working so well that we decided to move on to a group of children from the third grade (eight- and nine-year-olds); they too responded eagerly, seeing immediately the importance of clearing their minds of doubt and panic, using the techniques for art and music. Very young children (six-year-olds) also benefited from the programme; their movements became quiet as they gently harnessed their energy. Power that usually dissipated into noise and constant motion was directed instead into constructive action and learning while the children were in the classroom. As we breathed gently, reaching into the depths of silence, I felt that we had started to touch together the 'still point', and, as we tuned into this centre of quiet, we could go on to carry out our best work.

## 'And I Did It!'

One eight-year-old wrote about her reaction to her performance in a New York test, in which her results exceeded all expectations:

Samantha

Before I started the test I took 3, breaths I
read the top: and took 3 other breaths. I
began to read. As I was reading, I heard
somebody say Samantha, Samantha, (I didn't
now who) Then I took 1 breath, I heard
it again another breath, When I got to
the 5th breath, I didn't hear anything All I heard
was myself saying you can do it, You
can do it,...

And I did It!*

Samantha was right, she did exceedingly well on that New York test and on various practice tests. In the 'zone' she could cut out irrelevant distractions, such as the voice of another child, and yet – like top athletes – she was aware of the positive feeling that everything was going to be all right. Relaxed and focused, she couldn't lose.

## Soar to Excellence

> A beautiful accomplishment takes a long time, ultimately involving lifelong consideration. A sage said, 'Keep it with faith, practise it with keenness, perfect it with faithfulness – then though the task be great, you will surely succeed.'[10]

* Samantha was in a class of eight- to nine-year-olds who were attending an after-school programme with Mary Spellman in an attempt to improve their grades so that they might reach the fiftieth or sixtieth percentile in the New York tests. The results showed that 80 per cent of these children achieved above this and half of those scored on or above the eightieth and ninetieth percentile. (These results cannot be said to be statistically significant as the sample was too small.)

For a while I had left behind the weary egos of the international sporting life, and walked with wonder into the world of the small child. Together we realised that dreams can be attained even within the limitations of certain physical and social conditions. We began to learn that we can all soar to excellence and at the same time feel more in control because it is our own 'Peak Performance' that gives us a true sense of fulfilment – not the idea of measuring ourselves against others. Whether adults or children, in all areas of life, we are all our own rivals and it is ourselves we must push to the very limit of our perfection.

# PART II

## The Art of Education

Brittany

In the morning I went to school before the test; I did my Breathing and I did the test and it was easy

Mrs. Spears walked in I knew but I was concentrating so much that I didn't remember that she was there.

# CHAPTER 2

## Keeping Focused in Study and Examinations

I learned to lose myself so effortlessly in the breathing that I sometimes had the feeling that I myself was not breathing but being breathed.

EUGEN HERRIGEL[1]

### Relevance of School and Study

For many young students, the future seems too distant and the relevance of school and study seems lost in the immediacy of everyday life. The lure of a job – any job – often seems much more attractive than homework and exams. Therefore, it is important for students, from time to time, to draw up some goals and to re-assess their motivation so that they can begin to realise the purpose of what they are doing. They can then work out where they are going and what they are hoping to achieve in life. The importance of boring routines and nerve-racking exams can, at that stage, be appreciated for what they are – a grounding for life, a basis to enable us to pursue careers we find enjoyable and engage in work in which we are really interested. It is our job, as parents and teachers, to help pupils and students to relate their studies to everyday life.

## Concentrated Study

It is very important to find a balance in life at the main educational stage of a person's development. Schoolchildren, in particular, have a very full timetable that does not allow them much control over their lives. It is necessary, therefore, to help them to achieve a balance between interesting hobbies and recreation, and essential homework and study. Many children spend much longer at their homework and study than is necessary because they find it difficult to concentrate. Ironically, if they learn to focus properly they need to spend far less time studying as their time will be used far more effectively. They can learn that shorter periods of more concentrated study will lead to extra time for other interests as well as a more effective approach to work in general. I met one particular student, Nicola, who described how, usually, she spent many unnecessary hours in front of her study books and knew very little at the end of that time. After working on the meditation programme, Nicola was pleased to find that her study periods were much shorter and far more efficient. She also began to realise that concentrating in class is preferable to day-dreaming. Pleasant though dreaming may appear to be, it actually leads to much longer periods of homework or study because the student has little idea of what went on in class. As students have to put in time sitting through lectures anyway, it is important that they use their class time to the full. Time is the one commodity which we cannot replenish. A tenth-century Zen monk warns us of this:

> I urge you not to throw away time, for it's swift as an arrow, fast as a stream.
>
> YUNG-MING[2]

One College student described how he really wanted to do well but how, most of the time in classes, his mind drifted off. Unfortunately, he was equally undisciplined in his study; this combination led to his failing the exams. College students may have more control over their time than those still at school but often they cannot cope with the extra freedom and the task of planning their own schedules.

## Like a Game

The older students I saw in Dublin and New York were encouraged to draw up timetables identifying how much study or homework time they would need to spend on various subjects. I suggested that they scheduled the most difficult subjects for a time when they were most rested. As a matter of habit, most of the students were leaving their least favourite or most difficult areas of study to the end of the evening. This meant that they rushed through their poorer subjects in a state of exhaustion and, as a result, spent less time – rather than more – on the very subjects where they needed extra effort. In general, more organisational skills and a different attitude would be of great assistance to many students. One particular fifteen-year-old student, James, had a very good attitude towards his more difficult subjects. He told me how, when he was studying the 'trickier' subjects at Gonzaga College, he regularly tuned into the 'flow state'. He saw these areas of his study as interesting and 'like a game'. Instead of spending less time on these difficult subjects, James spent as much time as was necessary because he viewed them as fun and as a challenge. Consequently, at that time, he performed to the best of his ability by switching naturally into the 'zone'. At a certain level, maybe the difference between students is often not one of intellectual ability but one of perception, attitude and the ability to tune into the 'zone'.

## Lifelong Benefits

> Sit still and disengage normal activities. Draw energy from the earth. Admit power from the heavens.
>
> DENG MING-DAO[3]

As part of the meditation programme, the students were encouraged to take a short break when they returned home from school and then carry out some relaxation training. This would enable them to refresh themselves before starting to study their most difficult subjects. Before each new subject, students were advised to push their books to one side and meditate for several minutes in order to clear their heads. By emptying their minds of all thoughts, except the task in hand, they could then gather all of their energy and channel it into their performance. They also learnt to do a short burst of breathing if they felt their concentration slipping at any time. This was in order to help them cope with any distractions or feelings of tiredness. In the words of a small child in New York:

You know how when you wake up from a good night sleep or nap that you sometimes feel energy is just pumping into you. Well it's [*sic*] almost feels like that when you breath [*sic*].

However, relying on some isolated patches of meditation is not terribly useful. It is important to make the meditation a lifetime study; only then can lifelong benefits be reaped. Just as athletes prepare themselves mentally for many months or years, until meditation becomes second nature to them, so also should students. Unfortunately, because the psychological side of such an exercise is so intangible, it is often completely neglected by many people in all areas of their lives.

## Starting Line

Helena

I did use the breathing in the test and it madd it very easy I hope to pass that test.

The idea of the 'Peak Performance' programme is that exams are to be treated in a similar way to a starting line in a competitive race. Short bursts of meditation should be used to control the pre-exam nerves. This is particularly useful during the period just prior to the start of the exam when the students may find that their minds are filled with doubts or dread about the contents of the exam paper. If, however, they can learn to compose their minds – keeping them relaxed but focused – their energy will not be drained away by distracting worries. This approach would also help when dealing with the desperation of last-minute cramming and revision because, in a state of quiet contemplation, previously learnt material would be more easily retrieved. Of course, none of this should be viewed as an excuse for laziness or lack of work.

Many years ago, I was discussing these concepts with a university colleague in the context of delivering lectures. She reacted with horror: 'Being in the right state of mind won't help if you don't prepare your lectures properly,' she exclaimed. That is obviously correct and the same principle holds true for any area of work you care to mention. Entering the 'zone' is only of benefit if you are already well prepared and have put in all the necessary groundwork. As I have stressed throughout this book, Zen meditation is no instant cure – neither is it a miracle or an excuse for laziness. When you have put sufficient preparation into your work, then – and only then – can you move towards realising your true potential at that time. As we all know only too well, however, the converse is also true: if you are not in the correct frame of mind, the amount of work undertaken in advance may be of little value.

## Memory Retrieval System

One man, Paul Bright, who was involved in archery, and was working towards a maths degree at the Open University several years ago, found that meditation acted as a 'creative release' for him. This meant that he could identify, more clearly, the connections required to find underlying solutions to mathematical problem-solving. He commented that in one exam: 'A lot of material which I had studied several months previously and thought was forgotten was available for use more readily – almost like the memory retrieval system in a computer.' Before each study session, he meditated: '... it helped to dispel any distractions and clear my mind'. After an hour or so, when his attention started to wander, it was possible for him to take a break, knowing that he could return to his work: 'I could recover my concentration with the use of the breathing techniques and start again to study more intensely.' This individual felt much more focused and in control with the use of meditation. He was able to identify connections and remember information with a clarity which otherwise might have been dimmed by worry and self-doubt. Last-minute cramming was unnecessary as his focused mind retrieved material easily.

Irish Olympic swimmer, Nick O'Hare, also meditates to clear his mind when analysing data in preparation for his PhD thesis. Originally, he was using the meditation programme to improve his starts and times for the Sydney 2000 Olympic Games, but he now finds that the many pages of data, which he produces in the course of his research, can be analysed more effectively with the help of his meditation techniques. Another adult student who used these techniques with good results was Veronica Griffin, the Irish wife of a New York lawyer. She returned to college when her children began to require less of her immediate attention. Any student returning to college after a long break may find it particularly necessary to concentrate on organisation and study skills. Veronica used the meditation programme for both of these areas and found it very useful. She used short bursts of meditation while driving into the college and also in order to stay focused throughout her lectures. Staying focused for study and class is not an easy task, especially when college is combined with the hectic life of a wife and mother amidst the hustle and bustle of New York.

## Programme for Life

I initially started working in the area of education because some of the athletes I was seeing had begun to use their meditation techniques to help improve their study and exam methods. As a result, I began to use the techniques with college and secondary school students specifically for study and exams. The first student I worked with was Katherine. She was a bright, articulate student who became physically sick at any form of excitement – positive or negative – including Christmas and birthdays. As she got older, stress symptoms began to affect her when exams were looming. We started working together to see if we could find a solution to this problem, viewing the symptoms as a distraction that could be dealt with in a similar way to the pre-competition nerves of an athlete. Soon Katherine was proficient at the meditation programme and she began to feel more in control of her mental and physical state. The following year she gained good results in her Leaving Certificate and was accepted into the Montessori course she had chosen. After working for some time she has now travelled out to Laos to work in the only Montessori school in that country. She is teaching English to Lao children and is responsible for the education of the expatriate children in the school. Another challenge for Katherine is the setting-up of a Montessori teacher training course in Laos.

## Life in General

I met Katherine again in Dublin before she set off for Laos and she told me how she was still using the meditation programme when she had to make major decisions or choices. If she is upset she meditates: 'It levels me out completely and clears my head.' Irish student, Sandra Conway, also used the meditation programme throughout school and college. Later, when working in Boston recruiting staff for Massachusetts General Hospital, she continued to use her meditation. She found that it helped to clear her mind and assisted her in making quicker, more effective decisions: 'When I've too much work I stop, calm down, centre myself and refocus to find what I'm looking for.' Katherine and Sandra are examples of how the meditation programme can be used as I had always intended – not only as a help for exams but for life in general.

## Confidence and Self-esteem

When I started working with students, it was immediately obvious that the meditation programme was affecting their general confidence and self-esteem in a positive way. This was a fortunate by-product of the programme. A young Irish student who was hoping to get into university, but had initially displayed very little motivation as well as a lack of concentration, worked hard at the programme. Her mother found that her daughter gradually started to adopt a different attitude; she was more relaxed and confident with people of all ages and she was much happier in general. The student herself suggested that her self-belief had improved as she was no longer plagued with ideas of self-doubt; she subsequently did extremely well in her exams.

Years later, when I started working with young children in New York, I also found that self-doubt and lack of self-esteem were major factors in their poor level of performance. By practising the meditation programme, the children began to feel more in control and happier about themselves – regardless of their age.

One young child in the Bronx, nine-year-old Cynthia, described how she used the techniques for school work and how her feeling about herself in relation to test-taking had improved greatly:

> Once I was getting ready for a practice test. I had no confidence in myself. Then I thought – 'I can do it.' Then something let me down. Then I remembered about what Mrs Spellman told us about our breathing and how it helped me. So I kept breathing before and after each paragraph. When I finished I felt good about myself.

Cynthia also performed very well; in fact, she achieved a level far above what was expected of her on the New York City tests several weeks later.

## I Can Do It!

I found it interesting that on many occasions – in different countries and in different areas of life – individuals often wrote down, in their descriptions of performance in the 'zone', the statement: 'I can do it.' This occurred with people who worked in sport, education and the creative arts. The results displayed by those who felt this way were invariably very impressive.

On other occasions, however, when they weren't in a flowing concentrated state of mind, telling themselves that they 'can do it' didn't work. True confidence comes from an inner sense that tells us we are capable of achieving something special at that time – it does not come from telling ourselves simply that we are the best or we are able to do something. It is neither noisy desperation nor arrogance; rather it is a feeling of intuitive calm and stability, a quiet knowledge that we are in control and not distracted.

It became very evident to me that the children who used the meditation programme developed, not only an ability to feel good about themselves, but also a stronger sense of pride in their performance. They were able to express openly this feeling of pride and satisfaction and try to help others to feel the same way. They were also able to accept that, although they might not be at the top of the class, they had still fulfilled their capabilities at that time – quite a feat at such a young age. This feeling of self-worth is an extremely important factor for long-term development. We realise that as we look around and see many young people emerging dissatisfied from a disinterested, impersonal educational system. Often, the void they feel is temporarily filled by drugs, alcohol or support from negative peer pressure. One young student pointed out to me that the main reason he was involved in drugs was that he was bored and didn't feel he was good at anything. He admitted that if he could feel a sense of worth he would prefer this 'natural high' to drugs. If we could use these methods to help younger children to start to fulfil their potential, in school work and creative areas, we would be sowing the seeds of future success and increased self-esteem in the older child. The 'natural high' of the 'zone' or 'flow state' is what we want our students to attain.

## Coping with Anxiety

It is generally accepted that one of the most common problems in exam-taking is that of feeling very nervous. Some feelings of nervousness are natural, and necessary, but if they get out of hand, they become a major problem. Many people find also that they begin to anticipate anxiety symptoms and consequently develop a 'fear of fear'. In order to deal with this, I believe it is necessary to help children develop techniques which would make them feel more in control. This I have done with the use of the meditation programme and I have found that, as a result, children can be trained to cope with anxiety – and, indeed, the fear of anxiety.

Another Irish schoolgirl, Rachel, who had previously been practising meditation to improve her studying for the Leaving Certificate, went into her first exam feeling very tense and anxious. When she first looked through her paper, she began to panic.

> I made a conscious effort to relax and do my breathing skills. I had a clear mind throughout my exam. I didn't notice any distractions around me and was totally involved in my exam.

At the end of the exam she described how she felt a great sense of achievement which '... showed in my results'.

This problem of anxiety is also shared by much younger children. Eight-year-old Suzanne, in the Bronx said:

> When I took the [practice] test I felt scared 'cause I never knew it was hard so I took my breathing and everything was all-right. 'Cause Mrs Spellman and Filisity helped tell us to breathe and relax I did good on my test. I got 39 out of 40.

Another student, Kristin, also felt nervous during her test. She started using the breathing technique: '... then I went through the test, then it was easy. When I got the test back I got 22 out of 24. I felt great.' Many other children also did much better than expected in their New York city and state tests, coping better with their anxiety levels by the use of the simple breathing techniques.

## Adapting the Techniques

Even the small children were able to adapt the methods of meditation. Very often, they started their tests without using their breathing techniques. However, soon they learnt that they could use the meditation when questions got harder or when they began to feel anxious. One boy, Andrew, reported: 'I didn't use it [the breathing] at the beginning; then I felt sick, I used it and felt better.' Andrew thus demonstrated that he could learn to control some of his physiological symptoms. Nine-year-old Vladimir explained: 'I started the tests and I got confused, then I meditated and improved my focus.' A lack of adequate focus was Vladimir's main problem but he was able to improve this as the test progressed. Another student, Brandon, didn't use the meditation until part of the way through the test: 'When I got up to the hard parts I used my breathing and when I used my breathing it really helped me a lot because it helped me to understand the reading test.' The children went on to learn that better results would be obtained if the meditation techniques were used consistently all the way through the test, regardless of the level of difficulty. It was, however, very interesting to see the children adapting the techniques at such a young age.

## Guided in their Work

Other children felt as if they were guided in their work; they felt as if the answers were already on their paper. One of the girls, Brittany, who did very well in her exams (far above average), practised the meditation every day before she started to work: 'I felt like I was full of air and I could just run the pencil on the paper like a racehorse.' My own son, Andrew, told me how, on one New York test, he had used the meditation successfully to tune into the 'zone' and he felt as if the words were sitting on the page and he was tracing over them. His teacher, Joanne O'Dowd Brown, told me that he had done very well on this test, answering questions with great clarity and insight. Nine-year-old Domenico told me how he used the breathing: '... in a test on March 19th, it worked and I felt like I knew the answers from the start of the test.' With a distraction-free mind, the children soon learned that they were all able to retrieve material to answer the questions easily.

## Challenge and Change

The students themselves quickly begin to feel more in control, both for their study and their exams. In actual fact, it is the parents and teachers who are often the most surprised at the resulting changes in attitude and performance. Many of the parents of the students I have seen were amazed at their child's new approach to their studies. This suggests that we may not have sufficient faith in our children's ability and motivation. As a result, we may be involved in self-fulfilling prophecies rather than actual encouragement. As parents and educators we need to work together to find interesting and relevant ways to challenge and change the attitudes of today's youth. Education does not end in the classroom and, in order to help children to take full advantage of their school work, parents need to work with them showing them the relevance of learning for life. In some cases, teachers and parents would use the meditation techniques themselves; this also helps students to feel more motivated. Teacher Patricia McAdam described how she used the breathing techniques during a lesson in her language arts class: 'Right before the lesson, I began the breathing techniques and found that I was able to collect my thoughts and deliver them more clearly.'

This personal use by a teacher was an advantage not only for her teaching methods; it also meant that Patricia could identify and discuss her own state of clarity of thought when she was teaching the children to concentrate during lessons.

## Peer Pressure

Peer pressure is a major problem for adults as well as children. We all feel nervous about the views and opinions of our colleagues. Georgia McManus, a teacher in New York, explained how she used the meditation to deal with this problem and to prevent herself from concentrating on avoiding errors rather than doing an excellent job. As a facilitator at a special education conference on learning strategies, she was usually very nervous. On one particular occasion, after finishing setting up everything, she did some meditation in the library. Her thoughts were particularly clear during the conference. Her flow charts were professionally produced on the blackboard; and she was very pleased with the results and excited, rather than apprehensive, about the prospect of running another conference.

## Procrastination, Preparation and Delivery

Advice on how to improve teaching skills generally was sought by a lecturer who was teaching at a New York college. His objective was to deal with problems of procrastination which occurred when he was in the process of preparing lectures. He found it difficult to settle down to the job and to maximise the effectiveness of his work. He was surprised at my suggestion that the meditation programme would work for all of his problems. Perhaps he should have realised that the clarity of mind arising from meditation, when correctly undertaken, would provide the ideal remedy for the problems he was experiencing.

To accomplish a task effectively and promptly, we must learn how to harness and direct our energy. To prepare a good lecture, it is necessary to generate a flow of pertinent ideas while keeping distractions to a minimum. To deliver a good lecture, one should always try to enter the 'zone' or 'flow state' – concentrating on the task in hand rather than the reaction of the audience.

## Meditation – the Key to Excellence

> Being able to enter flow is emotional intelligence at its best; flow represents perhaps the ultimate in harnessing the emotions in the service of performance and learning.[4]

Usually, my work in New York involved students who were either not very well motivated in their school work or those who were just too nervous to perform well. It was, therefore, very interesting to receive a letter from a well-motivated student who was doing very well at school and had no particular problems. He was, however, still interested in using the meditation programme. Thomas Foley was a fifteen-year-old student at Regis College, the prestigious Jesuit high school in Manhattan. He had attended a talk I had given about the power of meditation and the 'zone' and was interested in seeing if these techniques would help him to achieve even better results at school. He sent me a letter explaining how he had used the 'Peak Performance' programme to attain an improved level of concentration in study and exams. He had, in fact, performed better than ever. He wrote:

> To prepare for an examination one must have total concentration while studying. Before I studied, I used the breathing techniques as you described in your lecture, especially on the night before an examination. I believe that by using the breathing I cleared my mind and kept the highest level of concentration possible. Whenever I felt I was losing concentration I began breathing and focusing my energy again. To ascertain results on your idea that the techniques could be applied to study, I used the technique during the third trimester of school. I ended up with Honors in every course and did very well on the final exams.
>
> On the night before, right before, and during the last German test of the year, I used the breathing techniques as you described. I scored higher on that test (a High Honors) than on any of the other eight tests of the year. This helped to solidify my trimester and final grade for German. I believe this was due to the total concentration I had while studying. With this significantly higher degree of concentration I performed at my peak ability. I ended up with a final course grade of or above Honors in every subject for the year, and I received the highest distinction for academics at my school.
>
> To summarize my findings, this is what I have found – Meditation is a mediation to higher concentration. By centering one's energies one can utilize those energies to their greatest potential. In the field of study this focusing of one's energies can be exercised on concentration, memorization, and application, the keys to study and education.

Thomas also realised that, although the use of the meditation for exams was indeed extremely effective, one of the keys to excellence was concentration in study.

## Immediate Gratification

> A massive tree grows from a tiny sprout; effective work gradually accumulated produces value and excellence.
>
> YUNG-MING[5]

In a public school in Boston, Dan Gorberg, a teacher, reiterated the need for improved concentration techniques when students were studying. Many of the children in his class suffered from short attention span, a problem that he felt was contributed to by the constant viewing of television; if the children don't like some programme on television, they simply switched channels. In class they behave the same way, tuning out whatever they find difficult or boring. The children attending Dan's school were not able to see any reason for school work, there was no value in it for them. What they deemed necessary was an instant result – immediate gratification. Like many of the public schools in New York, there were various emotional problems among the pupils in Dan's classes. The children's minds, unfortunately, were often cluttered with a lot more pressing problems than school work. Many of the children's fathers were in jail, or their parents were on drugs; deep-seated poverty was a way of life for most of them. A sympathetic teacher, Dan was aware that emotional issues come out in learning problems but, unfortunately, teachers rarely have the time or the training to cope with this.

Dan's sister, Sharon, worked at the opposite end of the social spectrum in a private school in Boston. She found that the majority of girls in her school were very self-motivated. On the whole, they were happy to attend the school and lack of concentration was not a major problem for them. Consequently, they were able to take advantage of the facilities made available to them. In the Boston public schools system, however, although large amounts of money were being spent on improvements, such as computers and new teaching methods, the children's concentration was usually so limited that these improvements were often of little value.

## Special Problems

The 'Peak Performance' programme has also been used, in New York, for children with special educational needs. One teacher, after listening to a seminar I gave, devised a programme to help the children to calm down before lunch breaks – a time when they were particularly hyperactive. The short bursts of meditation relaxed the children as they were standing in line and helped them to become more focused and less distracted.

In one class, I saw a group of children who were regarded as poor readers and it was thought that they were not able to comprehend much of what they were reading. Part of the problem seemed to be that some of them were silently reading so slowly that they had forgotten what had been read by the time they came to the end of the sentence. Their reading and comprehension were improved by inserting bursts of breathing at the beginning of a text and thereafter throughout the passage. This calmed the children down and helped them to remain focused. They were then encouraged to skim through these passages, meditating from time to time. Their reading started to speed up and their comprehension began to improve.

## Speech Therapy

Several years ago, the 'Peak Performance' meditation programme was also used in Britain and Ireland, with initial good results, to help treat speech and behavioural problems in youngsters. One young boy I was working with was having problems as a result of a stutter. This was especially pronounced in his Irish language classes. Con-sequently, whenever he was about to speak Irish he became extremely nervous as he worried about the possibility of stuttering – a resulting stutter thereby became inevitable. He was introduced to the meditation programme and taught to focus on the meditation rather than on himself and his own anxiety. Using the meditation techniques, his stuttering began to decrease. Following on this, the meditation programme has been used with success in various parts of the world. Any problem area that involves a stress component would be helped by the programme; as would any area in which improved focusing, a feeling of increased control and self-esteem play a part.

## Generalisation

One of the difficulties involved with the implementation of any programme is that of generalisation when applying it to areas outside of where it is being practised. This, of course, is a problem which arises in many different types of therapy. Although individuals might show some improvement with the therapist, when they return to an external situation, such as home or school, this improvement tends to drop off. It is necessary, therefore, to make the programme as interesting and relevant to life as possible in order to aid generalisation to other situations. The use of examples from the experiences of sports people often help in these circumstances, especially for children. I found it very useful to use the stories of some of the Olympic athletes with whom I had worked, as examples. The children could then identify this state in their own sporting activities and sometimes they used the techniques for sport alongside their use for study. As the 'Peak Performance' programme is seen to be an instrument for enhanced living, rather than for individuals with problems, there is often a more widespread enthusiasm for this than for other forms of therapies in these areas.

## Group Settings

The ideas behind the programme have been found to be useful at all levels and stages of education. However, its effectiveness can be enhanced further by involving the co-operation of parents, teachers and peer groups when implementing the programme. Small informal group settings are also useful; here students can discuss their results generally and see the results of other students – as one nine-year-old child in New York said:

> I would tell them it could improve your work and it could help you feel relaxed and calm. Also it could make you more focused and it will help you feel more confident in yourself. I would call it, 'Steps To Success'.

In the Western world, we are not generally taught the benefits of meditation – we often stumble on them ourselves and not always in the most constructive way. Teaching meditation in school, therefore, could be useful not only to gain immediate advantage but also to show how it can be used as an effective tool for life.

Breath is the thread that ties creation together.

MORIHEI UESHIBA[6]

One student, who felt great benefit could be gained from the concept of meditation, was seventeen-year-old Jane. At first, she found that the required disciplined approach was not easy, but she persevered: 'As time flew by it became an everyday task – I meditate every morning before school.... It's amazing to think that everyone has this skill and yet they don't learn how to use it.' In the Orient, meditation is a way of life reaching back through a long tradition. Tsai Yi-ching, a friend of mine from Taiwan, told me how, as a child, she was taught to meditate in school by regulating both posture and breathing so that she could achieve effective concentration. Such training has carried over into her adult life. Maybe soon meditation will be part of the curriculum of schools and colleges, both East and West.

# PART III

## The Creative Zone

After I did the meditation, images, creativeness and ideas came to me. Everything was going my way as if I was doing nothing. My actions were beyond my control.

MATTHEW, ELEVEN-YEAR-OLD STUDENT
ST JOSEPH'S SCHOOL, BRONXVILLE, NY

# CHAPTER 3

## The Creative Spirit in Art

I can tell you right now,
there are no secrets.
There's no mystery.
There's only common sense.

OREN LYONS
FAITHKEEPER OF THE NATIVE AMERICAN
TURTLE CLAN (ONANDAGA)[1]

### Perfection of Action

The modern words of Native American wisdom mirror the ideas of the ancient Chinese Taoist sages and Zen masters. Over two thousand years ago, Chuang Tzu told the story of a craftsman who was commissioned to make a bell stand for the King. After fasting for several days and ridding his mind of thoughts of glory and gain, the craftsman went into the forest to search for a suitable piece of wood. Before long he came upon a tree in which he saw the bell stand. He had found the perfect tree with which to work and was able to complete a perfect piece of art because his mind was free from distractions and greed.

He received great praise but denied that the finished work was in any way miraculous. There was no secret, no extra-ordinary power involved in his craftsmanship, just training, hard work and a composed mind – an 'ordinary mind' as the Zen masters tell us. It is in this state of mind that we see all things with great clarity. Not distracted by our own ego, we are able to see and to grasp opportunities which we may otherwise miss.

The Irish crossbow champion, Richard Delaney, is also a carpenter, whose daily work is truly excellent. Richard, however, finds it difficult to tell people how to copy what he does. Like all master craftsmen, his work is largely intuitive:

> I cannot tell my students how I carry out my work. I just tell them to watch me and they will see it manifest itself. The feel of the wood tells me what to do, I can't explain it verbally. I love what I am doing, time flies, I look at my watch and time has passed too quickly.

In his quest for excellence Richard will probably never be a wealthy man because he spends so much time on each piece. He is, however, a truly special person who believes that riches are found in contentment and perfection of action.

> If you know peace, then you thrive; if you know contentment, then you are rich.[2]

## Peak Experiences

Many years ago, I found that the results of the initial sports programme, which I had arranged for athletes, began, as might be expected, to show beneficial results in all areas of life for many of those involved. With this in mind, I then started to use the concepts embodied in the programme as a means of therapy to alleviate stress and other physical and psychological disorders. I soon found that my work was yielding equal success in the areas of both sport and health and that the results were proving to be interesting and positive. I then decided to move on to work with individuals involved in creative projects. Results in this area proved to be just as effective.

To live creatively is probably one of the most rewarding things we can do. Creativity can provide great harmony and balance in our lives. Sadly, the peak experiences of creative living are very often avoided out of fear. It is much easier to go along with the established pattern of our lives rather than opening ourselves up to potential ridicule or criticism. It is frightening for us to set off on a different, innovative path as there is always the possibility of failure. It may be much easier not to try at all rather than to risk failing and to lose our self-illusions.

The possibility of success can be equally fear-provoking. One top Irish cyclist suggested: 'If I don't do well, people will be sympathetic and I can always try again. If I get to the top there will be nowhere else to go and people will be waiting for me to fall.' Many individuals are afraid of being successful because of the changes it may bring about in their lifestyle. To avoid the challenge of creativity for fear of what may result is not, however, the answer to this dilemma. The important point is to know you have done your best regardless of the opinions of others.

## Creative Diminution

> Insist on yourself; never imitate. Your own gift you can present every moment with the cumulative force of a whole life's cultivation; but of the adopted talent of another, you have only an extemporaneous, half possession.
>
> RALPH WALDO EMERSON[3]

Most creative individuals, at some time in their lives, fear a lessening of their creative process and productivity. Sometimes creative diminution may occur at a time when we are undergoing major changes. We may need to accept this for a time and not resist it; as the martial artists of old used to tell us: 'timing is everything'.

Initiative behaviour, formed by thought of gain or glory, will also hold back our creative process. True creativity can only emerge when the individual is in a distractionless state of mind, totally enveloped by a love of the work that they are undertaking at the time. In order to achieve our best performance, therefore, we have to forget ourselves. We must relinquish our self-doubt and let go of both our ego, and our desire to succeed.

In sport, when achieving excellence, the athlete is relaxed yet alert, tuned in to every relevant stimulus yet unaware of any irrelevant distraction. The archer must be aware of the direction and strength of the wind as this affects his shooting. He must not, however, be clinging on to thoughts of winning or losing – or be distracted by the sight of the world champion standing on the line beside him.

## Union of Solitude and Silence

> Those who study Zen should be mentally quiet twenty-four hours a day.
>
> ZEN MASTER DAHUI[4]

This idea of tuning out irrelevant stimuli is not only in the domain of sport, however. John, a ninety-two-year-old man in Waterbury, Connecticut, described to me how being in the 'zone' improved the quality of his life. He had recently started art lessons at the nursing home in which he was staying. His response to his art was fascinating and very similar to that of a focused Olympic athlete. Despite being quite deaf and having problems with his peripheral vision, he had produced some amazing water colour paintings although he had no previous knowledge of – or interest in – this art form. He described how he set out purely to think of the job that he had to do. Although eight or nine people might have been sitting around the same table he remarked: 'I don't even know anyone else is there, I don't even see them.' He went on to say how happy he was to feel that way, lost in the creative process of his art. He was also glad to be doing something to pass away the time, and in particular to get away from the sickness surrounding him. In the 'flow state' he had found a way both to achieve beauty and to cope with the problems of sickness and ageing.

The Impressionist painter Claude Monet came close to describing the 'flow state' when he remarked that he wished to paint like one of the monks from past centuries who illuminated the old books in Europe. 'They owe everything to the close union of solitude and silence, to a passionate and exclusive attention akin to hypnosis.'[5] The monks, both scribes and illustrators, worked very long hours. The task was tiring as they painstakingly illustrated or copied out page after page of manuscript. There was no room for sloppy workmanship or mistakes. To us in the modern world, their work might seem tedious but the monks didn't appear to find it so. For most of them it was a rewarding, exciting journey – a point of union with God. Together, the monks worked to produce the finished product – pieces of outstanding beauty such as the Book of Kells, an illustrated book of the Gospels that was produced in about 800 AD and which is now on display in Trinity College Dublin.

## Strength and Vitality

Such dedicated illustrators and scribes appear, of course, in every culture. One such modern Sufi calligrapher, Ustad Abdolrasouli, with whom I studied in Tehran, awoke at three o'clock each morning, washed, said his prayers and then settled down to copy out part of the Koran or Sufi poems in the most beautiful Arabic script. Although in his eighties when I knew him, he rarely seemed tired and calligraphy continued to be a great source of joy to him. He seemed to gain hope and strength from his work in those early days of violence during the Iranian Revolution, even though his calligraphy had been removed from display in the Tehran Museum of Modern Art following the departure of the Shah.

After I left Iran, his son Soleiman sent me a page of the Persian Koran which Ustad Abdolrasuoli had written and which had been commissioned by UNESCO. The calligrapher had been quite ill but his writing portrayed the strength and vitality of youth and health. Like the monks of old, he viewed his writings as both a work of art and a communication with God (Allah). The medieval monks tell us that:

The parchment on which we write
Is pure conscience
The knife that scrapes it
Is the fear of God
The pumice that smooths the skin
Is the discipline of heavenly desire
The chalk that whitens it
Signifies an unbroken meditation
Of holy thoughts.

## Changing Light

For Impressionist artists, such as Claude Monet, nature was a source of wonder, a source of inspiration for work and life. Monet was inspired by the constantly changing beauty of nature in a way that is very oriental. In his landscapes the ever-changing light casts a glow and creates a sense of renewal. His work develops the idea that nature is not static and immutable but has a beauty that transcends time, transforming from hour to hour as the light changes. This theme was echoed by Lin Chang-Hu, a famous artist and calligrapher from Taiwan, who recently held an exhibition in Dublin. He described his art in the following way: 'I have a strong desire to paint the land in which I live, in the different seasons and in the changing light and shade of the day.'

For other modern-day artists, nature may not be the main influence but the serenity of solitude is still of great importance. One professor from Parsons, the famous New York fashion design school, described how she too felt that: 'Creativity comes from calm inspiration.' For her, creativity just didn't happen instantaneously, it was an interesting sum of many experiences of which nature was only a part. Inspiration might arise from some relatively mundane sight, a strap hanging in the New York subway, the sight of a bow tied at the neck in an unusual way. Everyday experiences such as these are capable of triggering off a flow of creative thoughts. When teaching in class in the 'flow state', she found that she transcended herself and was more in touch with the class. This resulted in better lectures as both she and the students communicated more freely, although she too acknowledged that this state, expressed in any intense way, occurs only rarely.

## Artistic Expression

> The Japanese calligraphers and *suiboku* [ink painting] artists spend quite a long time producing a perfect tone of black for their artistic work. Once their brushes touch their paper or silk, they feel more or less as if their work is completed.
>
> YOSHI USHIODA[6]

In ink painting the preparation time mentioned in the above quote is also a time for composing the mind. The gentle circular movement of the ink block against the ink stone clears away distractions as the artist prepares to 'attack' the rice paper. The artist's energy is harnessed – totally focused in action, on the task in hand, not dissipated by thoughts and doubts.

There is no hesitation when the ink painting is started. In fact, because of the nature of the porous paper or silk, any hesitant stroke means that the picture is spoiled. Strong, firm strokes are executed as if nothing else exists, as if one is facing an opponent in the martial arts, and consequently as if one's life depends on each stroke.

## Distracted Mind

> The magic of the Void is expressed in these paintings, bewitching the eye, summoning a mood of reverence.
>
> EUGEN HERRIGEL[7]

When I began to study *sumi-e* (ink painting) in White Plains, New York, with Nanae Momiyama, at first I strained and tried too hard, not able to relax, forgetting perfection of mind, only wanting to succeed. I would try to paint the lovely, simple orchid. Boldly I would paint the first slender leaves, and then as I realised that I had developed some degree of success, I would falter, afraid to go on. Next I would paint the flower and stem of the orchid, muscles tightening and tensing as I progressed, realising no touching-up or erasing was possible on the special paper. There before me would be a smudged or crooked stroke, visible proof of a distracted mind, a mind concentrating more on the need for success or fear of failure, than on painting.

One westerner, Margot Bohl, who became an accomplished Zen artist, painted bold black ink brush strokes against a white sea of space. One day Margot too showed how talent can be blocked when the pure love of painting is displaced by the need to achieve a specific goal. Margot had been planning to paint me a picture on my departure from Japan but she had not been able to complete her ideas. After we met for lunch one day, she returned home, emptied her mind of distraction, and produced an exquisite ink painting of a bird perched on a rock. This is a painting composed of strong strokes, full of vitality which I shall always treasure, not only as a wonderful piece of art, but as a memory of our meetings and friendship over the years.

## Core of Being

> The Zen mind, enlightened and disciplined is able to rise above mere technical ability and goes straight to the core of being.[8]

A student might ask if this approach to Zen painting has any relevance to Western art. Oh yes, indeed it does! Mental composure plays a significant rôle in everything we do – if only we could realise it. The boxer, training many hours a day for many years, may lose a medal, not because of his skill but because of his distracted mental state. The business executive may lose a deal, not because of his lack of experience and ability, but because, trying too hard to negotiate, he allows his mind to become cluttered and misses opportunities. So too in art the child or the adult must let go of thoughts of succeeding or of impressing others, and tune into the centre of their creative spirit – still and calm. Nine-year-old Jack explained: 'I tried to draw a Ninja. I couldn't do it. Then I breathed, I focused, and was able to draw it.' When we are too involved with the self, too involved with results, we try too hard. As the *suiboko* painter tells us, we can surpass our training and add another dimension by going 'straight to the core of being'. Of course this doesn't mean that we do not have to learn to train and to practise with great dedication, but rather it means that once technical ability has been acquired, we must transcend even this training in order to achieve perfection.

## Silent Centre

> The painter who is going to paint a bamboo must, before taking up his brush, sit in contemplation until he feels himself completely identified with the bamboo.[9]

In the 'zone', we are in a state in which everything is calm and flowing; everything feels so right, and then we touch the silent centre of perfection – we become the object we are drawing, no boundaries are distinguished. In this state of mind we can, at last, really see what is in front of us. Instead of drawing what we think a cat looks like, we look and see properly what is before us.

Mark LaRiviere, the art teacher at public school PS 97 in the Bronx – himself a well-established artist in New York – told me how he had been attempting to teach the young children to see properly and, as a result, to draw what they saw. He showed me a sheaf of art papers, some childish, others bearing the rudiments of sophisticated art work at a very young age. He told me that one particular child was drawing very well but halfway through she appeared to get tired, or bored. She stopped drawing what she saw and reverted instead to a childish form of art as her work progressed. Mark had been trying out breathing techniques over the years to help loosen the art flow. When he realised I was involved with similar methods in all areas of the children's school work he began to employ the same techniques as I had been using so that we could work together. He felt that the meditation may help the children to 'see' and consequently draw as they really saw. Several of his young students found that they used the meditation when it was difficult to draw various scenes. One of them, Keith, explained: 'I draw better now I have the breathing – it's easier.' Another student, ten-year-old Paul, felt: 'I do art tattoos better with breathing.' Another boy, Simon, used meditation to alleviate boredom: 'When I'm in art and I get bored, I meditate and it helps me keep going.' He and Michael also used the breathing when they went for an interview at the School of Art. Michael described how: 'At the interview I had to draw a fantasy animal, at the beginning it was difficult but after breathing it was easier.' Both children found that keeping their mind free from the distraction of doubt and worry helped to calm them down and to keep them more focused on the job in hand.

Meditation for these children in New York led to an increased clarity of mind. As they were feeling less nervous or distracted, they were able to tune more frequently into the 'zone'. They also felt that there was the extra psychological advantage of feeling in control and having a technique that works rather than being subject to the whims of fate.

## Facial Expressions

Since he was very young, my son, Andrew, has been adding facial expressions to some of the simple figures in his first books. Eyebrows denoted anger or surprise, mouths showed happiness or sadness. It was easy to realise that he really looked at the world around him, and still does. In my own case, art was my least favourite subject in school and I was accustomed to coming last. One day during an exam I was looking around desperately for inspiration. I looked up, and through the skylight I saw a single swallow swooping low over the school roof. Entranced by the slender body outlined against the mass of clouds, the graceful wings and curved tail, I drew the bird as I truly saw it. Maybe on this occasion I was so moved by the beauty of the swallow that what was normally a chore changed as I forgot myself, entered the 'flow state', and became the bird. Many years later I still remember that occasion very clearly and, like the athletes I was to work with later in life, I knew I had done well regardless of the result (in fact I got my only good mark in art in my whole school career).

On that occasion I stopped trying too hard. I forgot about the exam and I let go of the need to do well. As Japanese artists tell us, the state of 'spiritual rhythm' can only be attained in painting when the artist forgets himself.

## Obsessed

One famous painter who indeed forgot everything when he was working was the Romanian painter Dimitri Berea. He has been called the last great Impressionist painter of the twentieth century and was so obsessed with his work that he was always missing his appointments or forgetting to eat. According to his wife, Princess Alicia Gurrielli, Berea was thrown out of his apartment onto the streets of Paris because he couldn't pay his rent. He was too involved in his painting to bother about the business side of his work. The consequences of this could be very uncomfortable, as he found out when he was evicted on at least five occasions in Paris. Berea, who was commissioned to paint the Coronation of Queen Elizabeth II, was once invited to Buckingham Palace for afternoon tea. His wife laughed as she told me how on his arrival, Berea was informed by the Queen that it was the first and last time he would be invited to the Palace, as he was four minutes late. In view of his previous record of timekeeping – including missing meals completely and being extremely late for most appointments and even his own wedding – Berea must have been quite bemused!

## Sympathetic Eye

The house we were renting in Bronxville, New York was owned by Princess Alicia and when we first went to view it, the walls were covered in paintings by Berea – glowing coloured oil paintings of Paris, pastel-coloured portraits of some of the crowned heads of Europe. Berea had died many years before but a sense of his vitality lived on in his art. This vitality can be seen too in the wonderful work of the great American artist and illustrator, Norman Rockwell, who captured the ordinary events of American life with such a sympathetic eye – the rumpled sock on the child's skinny leg, the delighted look on the face of local gossips, not to mention the special mosaic of all the races hanging in the United Nations building in New York. All of this helps us to see into Rockwell's soul, a soul which belongs to everyone, a soul which tunes into universal themes understood and loved by all.

## Spirituality

Native American painter, King Kuka, touches other universal needs. He paints in an Impressionistic style, translucent colour diffused across the page, his work transfused with the spirituality of his own culture as he attempts to excel, painting from the heart as he tries to find himself. Maybe, although we sometimes don't realise it, we all spend our lives trying to find the meaning within ourselves. Very often this search preoccupies us and we realise, too late, that life has slipped by. Some try to fill the gap with a quest for ever-increasing amounts of money; others turn to drugs or alcohol or start a series of endless affairs. To fill this gap, to find ourselves, it is important to find more fulfilling ways which truly lead to calm self-transcendence. One way is to develop our creative ability for the correct reasons; another is to help others – in either case, we transcend 'the self'. The great psychiatrist, Victor Frankl, talked of this when he described happiness as a by-product of being dedicated to a cause which transcends 'the self' or being dedicated to other people. Two people who immediately come to mind when I say this are my teacher, the old Sufi calligrapher, and a French Catholic nun who looked after the lepers in Tehran. Both of these people, living in a place and time full of problems, were to become a life-long inspiration to me and were major factors in my enjoyment of my five-year stay in Tehran during the early part of the revolution in Iran.

## Past Glory and Achievements

> Your fear of death is really fear of yourself: see what it is from which you are fleeing!
>
> JALĀLU'L-DIN RŪMĪ[10]

I studied Persian calligraphy for four of those five years with Ustad Abdolrasouli. Every lesson was a delight and the atmosphere of his home was imbued with a sense of calm and renewal. Although he had been both a high-ranking official in the oil company and the most famous living calligrapher during the reign of the Shah, he seemed quite content to spend his latter years quietly producing beautiful works of art from the Koran and the writings of famous Sufi poets. His Sufi religious values, his search for artistic perfection and his love for his family and friends carried him through the turmoil and violence of the revolution. Life for him was lived in the present – not clinging on to dreams of past glory and achievements. As a result of this attitude he continued to produce works of great artistic merit until well into his old age. His infectious generosity of spirit and joy in life proved that being talented and famous doesn't need to make an artist selfish or arrogant. Had he behaved in an egocentric approach, his work would probably not have endured.

# Selflessness

This giving approach and love of life was also reflected in the work of Sister Maryam, a French nun in Tehran. After the revolution in Iran, leprosy, which had been previously eradicated there, became common again. Sister Maryam and the small group of Sisters in her order (founded in Algeria by Charles de Foucould) spent their days tirelessly helping to alleviate the hunger and suffering of the lepers. There were extreme food shortages for everyone in the early days of the revolution and for the poor and sick, life was particularly difficult. The wives of the foreign diplomats were impressed with Sister Maryam's work and rallied to her cause holding bazaars in various embassies to raise funds. It gave meaning to lives usually filled with tedious rounds of swimming pools and diplomatic parties.

When my husband and I finally left Iran, driving back to Europe by car, we went to visit one of the leper colonies in the north of Iran near Tabriz. Here we had the opportunity to watch those suffering from leprosy make their brightly coloured slipper socks and other handicrafts and meet some of the people who worked and lived in the camp. Sister Maryam may not have considered herself to be artistic or talented but her whole life was one continuous creative project. Her actions and her life inspired and affected others in a very profound way.

Having found themselves in their life's work, Ustad Abdolrasouli and Sister Maryam continued in their quest for growth, despite the terrible difficulties surrounding them. Throughout their lives they were able to transcend 'the self'. By touching their inner soul, they were able to reach out to others. We too, in our search for creative meaning in our own lives, can learn the strength of transcendence – by losing ourselves we gain perfection.

## Out of Balance

> Most great painters create their work unconsciously. That is the activity of true art.
>
> TAISEN DESHIMARU[11]

Just as a writer must write from the heart or his work is of little value, so too the painter must paint with true passion. Lifeless imitation or the search for commercial success can only result in inferior art. Success hopefully will come but as a result of good work. Of course, as a student starting off, each of us has to be prepared to learn from others and some imitation is necessary at this stage. We must always, however, tune into our unique creative spirit which will not remain quiet if unused and may in fact cause disturbance in our lives. The well-known Irish Jesuit and writer, William Johnston, once told me: 'If I don't write I get sick.' I feel that this is probably true for a lot of people; if they don't find meaning in life by using their creative talents their life gets out of balance; they stagnate and often suffer from psychological or physical problems.

I find, that in therapy, one of the most effective ways to help individuals to bring about change in their lives is to concentrate on helping them to develop their creative abilities. Then they can channel their energy into the 'flow state' and lose themselves in whatever they are doing. This is not just 'feeling good' but living with creative meaning. Most people with whom I have worked have some creative ideas that they wish to try out and at which they often wish to really excel.

They have procrastinated, however, waiting for the ideal time – a time that may never come. When they finally listen to the quiet of their inner voices with the use of meditation, they begin to feel calmer and stronger and any problems or resentments are seen in a different light. The situation may not have changed but by living creatively our attitudes and perceptions of difficulties often change. Victor Frankl, who was one of the most effective psychotherapists of the twentieth century, suggests that you cannot gain happiness by searching for it; happiness is a by-product of living with meaning.

## Cults and Isms

Georgia O'Keeffe, one of America's most unique artists, was not afraid to develop her own ideas. She acknowledged: 'I dislike cults and isms. I want to paint in terms of my own thinking and feeling.' She used incredible colours, unusual shapes, bleached shells, bones and flowers, and painted on a huge scale in order to make New Yorkers sit up and take notice. 'Most people in the city rush around so they have no time to look at a flower. I want them to see it whether they want to or not.'[12]

And notice they did – a style and colouring uniquely hers. The brilliant colours – the reds and golds, the blues and greys – reflect the influence of the painted deserts and mesas standing stark against the endless light of the skies of New Mexico, where Georgia O'Keeffe lived for a significant part of her life.

## Splashes of Colour

I visited the lovely adobe-style house of Mabel Dodge Luan in Taos where Georgia O'Keeffe and D.H. Lawrence had stayed.

I walked with my husband and children in the sage-green grass at the foot of the Sangre Cristo hills – grass highlighted, like an artist's palette, with splashes of colour from the wild flowers. I too fell in love with New Mexico, a place where silence hung heavy on the scented air, where time stood still and where art and poetry pervaded the atmosphere. I bought a box of beaten silver made by a local Native American artist in the gallery beside the Dodge Luan house. This was a gallery full of polished stone and wood sculptures, a pared-down style – simple yet stunning – reflecting the spirit of the Native American ethos and Japanese Zen, a harmony with nature, a closeness to the earth.

> The Great Spirit is in all things; he is in the air we breathe. The Great Spirit is our Father, but the earth is our mother. She nourishes us; that which we put into the ground she returns to us ....
>
> BEDAGI (WABANAKI)[13]

## Changes in Lifestyle

I first started working with artists ten years ago, when Siobhán, a well-known and accomplished Irish painter whose work I was already well acquainted with, rang me one day. She asked if visualisation techniques might work in order to cope with the distractions brought about by changes in her lifestyle and attempts to change direction in her work. In our meeting, we discussed excitedly the concepts involved in these areas. Although I had not used my 'Peak Performance' techniques with artists before, we were both of the opinion that they would be equally useful in this area. Together we examined the psychotherapeutic concepts and, as might be expected, we found that Siobhán was no longer enjoying her painting. She did not see her work as a challenge at that time and did not feel she was fulfilling her potential any more.

## Passing of Time

Siobhán left at the end of the session re-motivated and ready to reorganise her studio and start painting again. Her enthusiasm had been re-awakened. She decided to organise her time more efficiently, to cut down on time-wasting phone calls and to keep a notebook which would help her to keep her ideas in order. By using the meditation programme, and starting to view her work differently, Siobhán began once again to achieve the 'zone' and to paint her best work. She then started to show people her new ideas which she was expressing in her latest painting. She realised that this was something she had not been willing to do since she had last been in the 'zone' with any great consistency, three years before. That is to say she was fulfilling her potential at that time and doing her best work prior to an exhibition. She was focused to such an extent that she could not bear to be away from painting. Unaware of the passing of time, Siobhán had to force herself to take breaks for meals. In the intervening years she had not wanted to show her work, nor had it been received with as much enthusiasm as in the past. Her recent work has, on the other hand, generated great interest as she has developed new colour processes and new techniques. She has diversified from her print-making, for which she was well known, into new creative areas. Like all good artists, Siobhán had started again to enjoy her work, forgetting all else when she is immersed in her painting.

## Breathtaking Skill

Enjoyment is essential in the achievement of excellence and I saw this so clearly one day at an art demonstration I attended at the home of Lee Ming-liang and Hsu Ming-chih. The art on this occasion was the short-lived beauty of vegetable carving. Lui Xialoli, a Chinese master chef, demonstrated the great skill required to turn the humble carrot and swede into a masterpiece of craftsmanship. Pieces of carrot flew as, with great speed and precision, he transformed vegetables into dragons and exotic birds. He told me how he worked from the heart because he loved his artistry so much. He was self-trained and his mastery reflected his intuitive skill. When carving, he keeps his concentration by thinking only of the task in hand.

> You will find yourself travelling unencumbered and free as a bird in the sky, always living in the Eternal Now.
>
> ANTHONY DE MELLO[14]

A similar skill and concentration was also demonstrated by a talented young graphic designer, André Devereux. He had worked with me over the years when he was studying for school exams, adapting the meditation programme for his own artistic work and later for his own successful business. When he came up against a 'brick wall' in his ideas he would meditate to clarify his mind and to help his ideas flow. He told me that for him: 'Ideas flew past and eventually they are assembled like the carriages of a train as the whole design ties together into a working concept.' He finds that visualisation is the key for deeper conceptual levels of design: 'You relax, meditate and then visualise the ideas in your head – your mind is like a computer processing these ideas.'

## Self-Transcendence and Solitude

> The hills are like shouts of children who raise their arms trying to catch stars.
>
> RABINDRANATH TAGORE[15]

Whether the subject is a young child at school or a famous sophisticated artist, the same themes echo time and time again. There are many good artists who paint for commercial reasons but the ones who touch perfection – the ones who listen to their inner stillness – are quite unique. We can see only too clearly, in their work, the importance of self-transcendence and solitude.

# CHAPTER 4

## Zen and the Art of the Written Word

When I take pen in hand to write
And thus my marshalled thoughts indict
By the Eternal Pen,
What magic numbers then
Flow from my fingers, what divine
And Holy words are mine.

HAFIZ[1]

### Mingled Soul with Mind

Six hundred years after his death, the words of Persia's most revered Sufi poet live on. We can learn much about the art of writing from the life and feeling expressed in his poems. In Sufi poetry, various themes of nature and mystical allegories were developed, all symbolising the unity with the Beloved, the Divine. The moth attracted and consumed by the flame of the candle was one theme, another was the love of the nightingale for the rose – devoted to its beauty, unaware of the pain of the ever-present thorn. The bittersweet beauty of nature was transcended by the wonder of the Sacred. To reach this stage of development in his work, Hafiz studied and developed his ideas for many years, and the passion in his writing is there for all to see. It is this passion that holds us so many centuries later; a passion in which he has 'mingled soul with mind', as too have Omar Khayyam, Rūmī and other famous Sufi poets. The very vitality of these poets' work, which blends themes of everyday life with mystical significance, has led to the literary importance of their poems – all written from the depth of the poet's universal soul.

## Stylised Words

Moving to another culture and another era, eighteenth-century Japanese Zen poet Ryokan also conveys to us how to write with meaning and vitality, how to touch our page with the Eternal Pen of Truth. He too was inspired by the beauty and sadness of nature all around him and he deals with the passing of time and the transience of life with a simplicity that says more than any sophisticated phrase ever could. It is this simplicity and sincerity that he advocates for all writers:

> But if you don't write of things
> deep inside your own heart
> What's the use of churning out
> so many words?

RYOKAN[2]

He highlights the idea that there is no point in producing fine, stylised words. These might sound clever, but as they are only imitations of another's thoughts, they turn out to be devoid of feeling. However melodious they might sound, they end up meaningless and hollow because they do not come from the heart of the poet or writer. If there is no emotion in the writer then there can be no response in the reader.

In New York I noticed that some of the young children who had experienced the most difficulty in their lives – such as death or violence – seemed to write with a greater depth of passion and feeling than others; in their sadness they touched the raw core of their being. Their anger and tears overflowed into their writing. One child, whose mother had died the previous year, gave me her school journal where she had recorded her feelings. The pages were filled with violence and hatred – a shocking level of vehemence in anyone, especially a child so young. The girls around her talked eagerly about their writing and I asked her whether she also wrote poetry. She shook her head sullenly. Later in the lesson she brought me a beautifully written poem that she had just produced. She then told me how the walls of her bedroom were covered with poems, written for her mother. The teachers, although usually very understanding, did not see her pain and hurt. They only saw a disruptive child. At this stage, however, the school principal, Janet Spears, began to take a personal interest in this child and, subsequently, the young girl began to improve at school.

It might be useful, as already happens in some places, to send volunteers into schools to spend time with such troubled children. The child does not always need to see a professional but may benefit from a caring individual who has time to spend simply talking and listening. This would relieve teachers who are already over-extended by their workload.

## Betrayal

I remembered the young New York girl, whose mother had died, when I was back in Dublin and I met street poet Tony Gill. He would sit everyday on the step outside the Oisín Art Gallery, on Westland Row, and would often ask me to copy down his poems for him. Tony wrote with a rawness of spirit about his experiences living and sleeping on the streets of Dublin:

> There shall be no stars tonight
> the sky is black
> like my heart is now
> Even when the sun rises
> it shall give me no warmth
> For I have lost faith
> in a friend I once trusted
> Death they say is final
> but betrayal lasts longer

These words express, with dignified simplicity, the hurt of his betrayal by a friend.

When alone in his hut Ryokan, the wandering Zen monk, wrote his poems and practised his beautiful calligraphy. He too let his words and thoughts flow freely, the sadness and loneliness, the joy and simplicity, all showing in his work – no greed or artifice as he lived each moment to the full:

> Like a drifting cloud
> Bound by nothing;
> I just let go
> Giving myself up[3]

Bashõ, who was probably one of the most renowned *haiku* poets in Japan, was also able to write from the depths of his soul and thus touch the reader because of this authenticity. Even though his words might, at times, sound less elegant than those of other poets, the resulting picture evoked by his *haiku* is powerful; as bathed in light, we feel the vitality, we sense the silence:

Autumn Moonlight –
worm digs silently
into the chestnut[4]

## Creative Writing

Just as Ryokan advises us not to imitate other writers' styles and to beware the man who 'copies the classic Chinese verse', so too does Bashõ tell us to be our own person. Both of these poets would feel at home in any creative-writing workshop at the turn of the twenty-first century. Bashõ tells us to learn from others to sense the spirit of the old masters but not to copy them blindly: 'Don't follow in the footsteps of the old poets, seek what they sought.'[5]

In our own lives we should remain open to others, while at the same time listening to our own heart and looking into our own soul; we should not be closed off by the confines of culture and education, of taste and fashion. So too should we learn from nature, from all the wisdom and energy that surrounds us. Like the famous Impressionist painter, Claude Monet, we should try to pursue the unattainable, we should try to 'paint the air'. To write of a tree we should become a tree, we should bend with the wind; to paint a leaf we should become a leaf, we should dance on the spring breeze.

## No Hesitation

In Zen painting there must be no hesitation, the paper or silk is such that there can be no retouching – each stroke is final. Bashō tells us that in writing, also, there must be no hesitation. Instantaneous, the strike of a pen and a thought is also laid bare: '... like a woodcutter felling a huge tree, or a swordsman leaping at his enemy'.[6]

Probably Bashō and Ryokan would be amused and delighted to read Ray Bradbury's book[7] on a Zen approach to writing, in which he suggests that we should relax and stop thinking when we are creating. He knows only too well that, trying too hard, we tense our body and dull our mind, unable to let our thoughts flow, unable to touch the centre, the still point of our creativity. Ray Bradbury tells us we must relax and let our creativity flow. Under this flow, suggests Bradbury, we uncover the individual, the unique person. It is from this unique spirit that true art springs. As we grow older we lose our childlike spontaneity, and with it much of our creativity, as we are programmed to move as smoothly as possible through the education system on an automated assembly line. We quickly learn that original thought doesn't fit in with systems, and we begin to filter any unusual or different ideas through the distorted lenses of censored thinking. As teachers and parents, we ourselves often cannot progress beyond the blockage in our own learning and, because of this, we cannot take a delight in our children's unique responses. Instead of praising any unusual way of seeing or describing objects and events, we hastily attempt to shuffle their thought processes back onto the straight and narrow path.

True original thought, however, is neither programmed nor limited. It expresses itself at unusual times, in diverse places.

It is often spontaneous and unplanned. In order to produce our greatest work we must return to unthinking, childlike behaviour. Putting our sophisticated veneer aside, we have to return to the spontaneous joy of the child.

## 'To Be'

> For you can look at things while talking or with a radio going full blast, but you can see only when the chatter stops.
>
> FREDERICK FRANCK[8]

Just as in drawing we use our eyes to look at objects but rarely really see them; so this same approach begins to affect the view of the world in which we live. In our cities of shopping malls and concrete buildings, we lose our powers of description as we lose touch with nature. As we all know, it is not so easy or meaningful for parents to conduct a study of the various shades of green in Bloomingdale's department store as it is in the forest or countryside. In order for the inner artist to survive we need silence not constant, mind-shattering noise. We need to rekindle the ability of the young child in us to see and to describe. We need to reach into our inner soul to bring out the original in us, not to produce the synthetic fad and fashions of the day. In this 'switch-on-switch-off' society of ours we rush helter-skelter through life, forgetting to stand and stare, and ultimately forgetting 'to be'.

One nineteenth-century American writer who learned just 'to be' was Henry Thoreau. He was a poet and philosopher who found inspiration in both solitude and nature. He was born in Concord, Massachusetts, a place where the old houses of writers Ralph Waldo Emerson, Nathaniel Hawthorne and Louisa May Alcott sit together on a secluded road. Thoreau built himself a hut on the edge of Walden Pond in 1845, a time that was probably his most creative period. Reading the account of his life at Walden Pond, it is easy to see why this might be so, as his are not just sentimental tracts on the beauty and vitality of nature. Thoreau develops a balance of practical sense and mystical spirit as he combines a description of his life, work and philosophical views with the wisdom of Greek and oriental thought.

## Present Moment

Thoreau embraces the present moment as enthusiastically as any Zen monk. His wish was: '... to stand on the meeting of two eternities, the past and future, which is precisely the present moment'.[9] During the first summer at Walden Pond he was engaged in manual labour – growing vegetables and building his hut. Sometimes he spent his days in timeless contemplation; he knew that this behaviour would be regarded by many as idleness, but he himself felt these occasions to be full of good fortune. Again the 'here and now' was of intense importance to him: 'There were times when I couldn't afford to sacrifice the bloom of the present moment to any work, whether of the head or hands.'[10] The ability to appreciate this state of just 'being' is a great gift. To divorce ourselves from activity is even less easy today, at the turn of the twenty-first century. Our lives are frenetic, complicated by action and a need to acquire ever more possessions, to search for a happiness which we never attain. We seem to have forgotten that out of contemplation comes a sense of peace and fulfilment. Out of our silent being our best work is produced.

Another writer who thrived and wrote prolifically in solitude and 'profound isolation' was Lafcadio Hearn.[11] For him the isolation came from living in Japan at the end of the nineteenth century – a time when very few foreigners lived there. A writer of Greek and Irish origins, he adopted the lifestyle and literature of Japan, while interpreting Western literature for the Japanese.

## Words Tumble Out

Many years ago Professor William Johnston, who had by that time written many books on the comparison of Christian Mysticism with Zen Buddhism, suggested to me what the secret of his success was. He wrote because he had something important that he really wanted to say. He remarked: 'When you have something to say, then you write a book.' This may not be the only reason for writing, but it certainly seems to be the most compelling. When you want to say something that matters greatly to you, the words tumble out one after the other as the obsession to write fills every waking moment. Victor Frankl, after his release from the German concentration camp, wrote down – in nine successive days – an account of his imprisonment and his theories on meaning in life; so came into being the basis for one of the most moving books of the twentieth century: *Man's Search for Meaning*.

Victor Frankl had intended this book to be published anonymously. He just wanted to depict the suffering endured by everyone in those camps and to show that meaning can still be found even in the most degrading situation. The fact that this book became such a success only further validated Frankl's ideas. His thought is very close to the philosophy of the Zen masters when he tells us: 'Don't aim at success – the more you aim at it and make it a target, the more you are going to miss it.'[12]

## Fluency and Flow

In a literary study that I carried out in New York to assess the effect of the 'zone' on children's writing ability, emphasis was not placed on brilliance of writing. Instead, the children were encouraged to focus and enjoy their work. In an attempt to increase the fluency and flow of children's writing, various teachers in New York began to use my meditation programme. Two teachers who were particularly involved were Patricia McAdam, who taught in a small private parochial school in the wealthy suburb of Bronxville, and Mary Spellman, who taught in a large public school in the Bronx. The school environments and socio-economic backgrounds of the children were very different. Nevertheless, both teachers were very alike in their dedicated enthusiasm and open-minded approach to providing the best facilities for their classes.

Although this was not intended to be a scientific study, the results were very encouraging and turned out to be similar in both sets of classes. The majority of the children produced interesting poems, pieces of prose or descriptions of the 'zone' or 'flow state', depending on their instructions. As Mary Spellman pointed out, some children who normally found it difficult to write even a sentence, managed on this occasion to write whole paragraphs effortlessly. In Mary's school one day, the children were asked to quietly practise the breathing techniques and then to write a half page on anything they wished. A concentrated silence reigned, then the children began to write – heads down, pencils flying over the page they wrote as fast as they could. Not all the writing was of a high standard. Some of the spelling and grammar left a lot to be desired but there was some good writing and a good flow of interesting ideas.

## 'The Wind Helps Me Live'

One child, who was not doing very well at her school in the Bronx, wrote of wanting to go home to talk to her mother. She wished to play and feel the wind: 'The wind helps me live.' Her fears came to the surface as she wrote about friendship, whether or not people liked her or whether or not she would start to learn faster. She wrote easily on a topic that she would find difficult to discuss normally. Another child described how:

---

I was all nurvis and strest
out uttill falist came and we
practis our breating stragsity
and I felt much ~~Better~~ when
we do our breathing it was dofently
bettar I felt relakes when I
did my breathing I felt like
I was in a feald of flowers
bocause I love flowers I
felt the feather ticklying me.

---

The spelling in this quote may not be so good but the feeling and ideas are wonderful and may help one to visualise the child sitting in the stifling humidity of a New York summer behind the bars of the schoolroom window. For a brief moment, she escaped to a faraway field full of flowers and was able to communicate this feeling.

In a very different setting, a lovely New York suburb surrounded by majestic pine and oak trees, Patricia McAdam's class was instructed to practise the breathing exercise and then to write a poem about nature. One girl, Julia, who was initially rather sceptical about the ideas, having missed the first lesson and explanation the previous week, described how:

My instructions were: 'Write as much of a poem as you can about nature after doing the breathing exercise.' I opened my eyes after the exercise, thinking there was no way this can work. I picked up my pen and didn't think. My pen ran across the page. I had produced a good poem without even thinking.

Julia was correct; her poem was excellent!

## 'It Shot'

The old Japanese *Kyudo* masters – referring to their archery practice – talked of 'it shot' rather than 'I shot', showing that when perfection occurs it must be seen as divorced from the self, otherwise the archer will not continue to improve. Writers too, talk of the pen writing by itself, a magical state which takes them by surprise as – unaware of distractions, the self forgotten – they achieve perfection. The children in the two New York schools found that by using the meditation they too were full of ideas and free from strain – their writing was flowing and natural. Eleven-year-old Catherine described how:

> When I use the meditation for writing, ideas quickly pop into my head faster than I can write them down. My mind is free of worries but full of vivid ideas.

After meditation another pupil, Jamie, also felt as if 'it wrote' and explained:

> When I write my poems, the state of mind always helps me out. It makes me focus on what is happening. Sometimes it feels like I am not doing my job.

After meditation, many of the children found they were thinking and writing with greater clarity of mind. As a result they were able to focus on the task. Often, just deciding what to write about is a problem, but eleven-year-old Jessica observed:

> I used the method once, and it helped me write a poem. The words just seemed to flow, that made me feel good because I was having trouble choosing a topic, and I did the breathing and everything came out like I wasn't even thinking!

Jessica let go and achieved a state in which she wasn't even aware of thinking.

## Words Spilling Across the Paper

> Alone
> The glistening snow
> falls upon my freezing cheeks
> like small tears of ice
>
> CLARE HOLOHAN, THIRTEEN YEARS OLD[13]

In a focused mental state, words flow at a tremendous rate, spilling across the paper, unchecked, unstoppable. On many occasions in New York, I heard the tap of keys as my daughter Clare's fingers flew over the word processor like lightning, words tumbling out faster than her fingers could go. When she had finished, I asked her about her state of mind. She smiled and said: 'I couldn't stop, everything was flowing.' On other occasions, the sound was laborious, hesitant, her fingers matching her distracted thought processes. Clare used to love to read, but was going through a period when she didn't read so much, yet she continued to write well. She wrote as she spoke – naturally and full of life – from her heart. She explained that she writes whatever she feels or sees, however silly it might sound. She doesn't write what she thinks other people might like to hear. Every word may not be correct but the overall picture flows with life and spontaneity. Clare wrote the above *haiku* in Patricia McAdam's class and it was originally entitled: 'Snowman'. It was a reminder of the many days she had spent playing in the snow in New York. When she returned to Dublin she retitled it and entered it in a competition.

Schoolchildren appear to experience this creative state more often than college students or adults. In my conversations with the Fordham University basketball team in New York, many players described how they experienced the 'zone' more often in high school than in college – both in sport and academic work. As we get older we become more afraid of sounding silly and, as a result, we keep our natural feelings and talent hidden. This holds us back in our achievements. Several years ago an Irish journalist described to me how he would sometimes write his columns in the 'flow state'. On these occasions his work was completed in a much shorter time than normal and with less need for correction and revision. He admitted that it was not very easy to ensure this desired state of mind and, in fact, he felt that he, like many others, only achieved the 'flow state' naturally, and on rare occasions.

## Gather My Thoughts

The initial attempt to get down to writing is often very difficult for everyone. At such a time, the thought of cleaning the house or any other chore may suddenly start to seem very attractive. On these occasions, it may be useful to build up a routine which helps individuals to focus and enter the 'zone' more easily and consistently. In New York, I developed a personal routine to help me to focus and to finish my last book on time. A friend of mine, Eve, gave me a lovely hand-coloured candle which she hoped would help inspire my writing. Every morning, I would sit at the table and meditate, gathering my thoughts. I would then light the candle. This worked very well until one day, in a 'flurry of flow', I cast aside my completed papers and nearly burnt the house down! I decided at this stage that the lighted candle would have to be an occasional extra.

I arrive at noon
bright sky, scudding clouds.
Speed up the avenue crunching gravel
a sentry of nodding daffodils.
Pale sunshine washes over the house ...

EVE

This is an extract from a poem Eve wrote one day, after she had used the Zen meditation programme. Eve had used the meditation very effectively in the past for visits to the doctor or dentist. This was the first time, however, that she had used it with her creative writing. She was under pressure to produce a poem for her writers' group and needed to achieve clarity of mind. She found it was much easier to achieve greater flow and fluency with the meditation.

## Writer's Block

One woman writer, who I met several years ago, came to see me because she was experiencing a block in her writing that was making her frustrated, bitter and angry. She felt her life was slipping away and she was no longer in control. Although she was very talented and had a pleasant lifestyle, she viewed the passing of time with a sense of despair rather than of accomplishment and fulfilment. She remarked:

> I haven't done what I feel is important. I want to use my life well but I feel it's slipping away.

She had begun to feel that her colleagues would no longer see her as talented and this contributed to her anger and turmoil. Her negative feelings were so strong that she began to resent any time that she spent with her children. The writer adapted the meditation programme to her own life and started again to focus and produce and publish fine pieces of writing. As she felt more fulfilled in her professional life, she found her relationship with her children improving simultaneously.

## Hierarchy of Needs

The feelings that this woman experienced are quite common and many of us can probably identify with this negativity – especially as we get older. We feel that time is slipping by and we may not have used our talents fully. Maslow describes in his hierarchy of needs how we strive for fulfilment when our basic needs are met. Sometimes it doesn't matter, however, what we actually achieve in life, it is our perception of our achievements that counts. One extremely successful American doctor, Lloyd, told me how he felt he hadn't made a success of his life – how he hadn't made a mark. This was despite the fact that he and his wife were very successful in their careers; he had subsequently become a millionaire and had also brought up three wonderfully talented children. Maybe one of the reasons for his malaise was that he had never really been sufficiently interested in his career, despite being very good at his job. That had been fine when he was young and intent mainly on financial gain; but as he got older it didn't mean so much to him. Overt rewards of status and money meant much less than a sense of inner meaning. This inner sense of fulfilment – invisible to others – was desperately sought by Lloyd.

He began to realise that something was missing in his seemingly successful life. He had taken up marathon running, and that had helped somewhat, but he felt he needed more. Working with an orthopaedic physician, he started monthly free clinics to help runners and walkers to deal with sports injuries or training and exercise problems. He subsequently began thinking of using his ideas to work with the homeless.

## Kaleidoscope of Fantasy Shapes

As parents and teachers, we can help to nurture this sense of fulfilment in young children by our attitude to their creative efforts. One day, when I sat in on a teachers' meeting in New York, a staff member complained about the terms used by a first grader to describe the moon. This teacher thought that the adjectives were contradictory and didn't sound 'right' – blue, heartless, cold, fire, smooth – yet I, and several other teachers, felt that the words were very vivid and by no means inappropriate, as did the teacher from Columbia University who was leading the group. Maybe the real point is that we often judge children on how well they fit into our narrow, conventional, descriptive system. Children do see and do describe objects and experiences differently from adults. What might be viewed by us in a fairly dry technical way may be seen by a child as an exciting, magical or cruel experience. The moon for a small child may be a kaleidoscope of fantasy shapes, forms and colours, whereas we may see the same object as a fairly ordinary mass of volcanic craters. This difference in our thinking processes often hinders us from encouraging and helping the child's imagination to develop.

## Child-like Wonder

> Moon above is alone
> Sit in solitude
>
> DENG MING-DAO[14]

How can we adults rekindle this state of child-like wonder, enhanced with the extra factual knowledge and experience of age? One way is by tuning into our creative centre – that still point which balances the meeting of humanity and transcendence. This is the state of perfection of mind that top world performers and small children refer to as 'magical'. These two groups may be worlds apart but they are united in their awe of the perfect process, the state of going beyond 'the self' and touching the realm of the infinite.

It is only at such a time that we do our best work and use our talents to the best of our ability. In the final analysis, only we alone may know we have done this. We may not have won a medal or prize but we ourselves can assess our own achievements. If we leave behind our distractions and ego, if we tune into the state of 'flow' or the 'zone', then we have become the best we can be. This appears to be a measure of whether or not we have achieved our personal excellence. Some adults don't recognise this mental state to any great degree and obviously there are different levels and intensities of the state. The fact, however, that we may not recognise this state may be regarded as positive rather than negative – there is so much more for us to achieve.

# CHAPTER 5

## Perfect Harmony in Music and Dance

In the East, the highest kind of music is that which sends the listener into *samadhi*. The silence which follows is an essential part of the music. The audience should be in the state of people who are watching the sun set into the sea....[1]

### Magic Spell

We can probably all recognise the state of silence outlined in this quote when we unite with perfection of different kinds, when any noise is an unwelcome intrusion which breaks the magic spell. One Montessori teacher in New York, Helen Marrico, recognised this description immediately as the silence of very young children in her classes, forgetful of themselves, totally absorbed in their tasks.

When I am writing or studying, I find that music often helps me to achieve a deeper level of concentration – although this doesn't, of course, apply to all types of music. The music of Beethoven or Mozart, in particular, helps me to tune into a creative flow more easily. Great composers such as these tune into the energy of the Infinite and help us to transcend everyday existence and acknowledge the perfection of the spirit. As a general observation, the music of the East may be considered more spiritual than that of the West. The music of India and Persia is used by the Sufis to enhance their meditation and communion with God, it is an expression of the beauty and harmony of the universe. Everything in the universe has its own perfect rhythm and timing. In Japan, music echoes the timeless beauty of nature. The sound of the traditional Japanese musical instruments echoes the silvery patter of the raindrops against the roofs of the old temples and the haunting whisper of the wind in the pines.

## Samadhi

Over the centuries, in all forms of mysticism from different cultures, music played an important rôle in helping to achieve perfect silence and union with the divine. Hazrat Inayat Khan, the famous Sufi musician who lived in the late part of the nineteenth and the early part of the twentieth century, suggested that it was easier to achieve perfect stillness or *samadhi*[2] by the use of music. He felt, like Bashõ the Japanese *haiku* poet, that we learn from the spirit of the master – not just from the words or the music itself. For Hazrat Inayat Khan, music was a depiction of the Beloved, of the Divine, and he felt that inspiration is a 'more elevated type of intuition' – which we attain by focusing our mind on the divine mind:

This phenomenon is so great and so wonderful that its joy is unlike any other joy in the world.[3]

So the beauty of the music is an outer reflection of the perfection of the soul. He goes on to say that the more we want to achieve perfection, or the more we worry about success or failure, the less likely we are to be creative. This too is something that many an Olympic athlete has had to learn the hard way. Hazrat Inayat Khan tells us that we cannot compose good music or write beautiful poetry by becoming anxious or by trying too hard. We receive true inspiration only when our minds are calm and unconcerned by thoughts of gain, only when we are ready to lose our selves and empty our hearts.

## Sense of Harmony

Over the years, I have worked with various musicians to help them cope with performance anxiety. Here again, a similar picture emerges to that found in the experiences of sportsmen and in the teachings of the Sufi mystic. Most musicians acknowledge that their best performances are achieved during periods of 'flow' – of self-transcendence – times when they are totally lost in their music and the instruments appear to play by themselves. More often, however, the musicians concentrate on the audience, or on their own desire to excel or to impress their peers, rather than focusing on the task in hand which is to concentrate on each note and to perform their music as well as possible. One musician (in a Dublin orchestra) was constantly afraid that he would be sick on stage or would feel compelled to make an embarrassing exit. Other musicians with whom I worked told me they were frequently fearful that they were going to make a mistake in playing the music. The obsessive fear of any of these eventualities obviously makes it more likely that such occurrences will in fact take place. Being nervous on stage is, of course, very normal. When carried to excess, however, it is rarely beneficial; as in sport, self-focusing can become intensified to the detriment of the performance. As a result, the musician is often distracted and the perfect sense of harmony, which comes from transcending the self, is lost.

## Control

Over the years, I have found that many of the athletes and coaches that I worked with were using the techniques of the 'Peak Performance' programme not only for their work in sport, but also in various other areas of their lives. Noel O'Reilly, when he was working as the coach of St Patrick's Athletic football team, described how the meditation helped him with his singing:

> On the occasion of the school carol service at Christmas I was singing solo; I began to panic just before I was due to go up to the altar and sing. I spent a few minutes breathing and visualising. That settled me down emotionally and my performance went very well because I felt in control.

This concept of being more in control is equally important in other aspects of life and, of course, especially in sporting activities. The thought that anything can happen, that life is unpredictable, is a frightening concept and puts enormous pressure on the individual who is preparing for a performance. Any technique that can reduce this lack of control, especially for musicians performing in front of an audience, is therefore of immense value.

Mihaly Csikszentmihalyi gives a description of this use of harmony as experienced by a musician who is in the 'flow state':

> I no longer notice my fingers, the score, the keys, the room; you become one with the music....[4]

Concentrating on their breathing and learning to trigger the 'flow state' has, in my experience, helped musicians to gain greater control and to overcome this frequently experienced anxiety. One musician, who rarely enjoyed his performances at important concerts, found that the meditation programme helped him to feel more calm and focused. On one occasion, after playing in a televised performance of Verdi's 'Requiem', he remarked that he had been able to control his nervousness and even to enjoy his performance. Once he was able to let go of his tension and distracting thoughts, his music improved. Touching the stillness of his quiet mind he could achieve excellence.

## Negative Chatter

The meditation programme can be utilised by music students of all ages and at all levels of ability. Catherine, aged twelve years, a young student in a Westchester school (in New York), realised that if her mind was calm she would sing more proficiently. There was, in fact, little difference between her self-doubt and the anxieties experienced by the older professional musicians. Instead of concentrating fully on her singing, she was too accustomed to focusing on the incessant negative chatter in her head. Using the meditation techniques made her feel considerably more confident:

> When I use the technique for singing I feel relaxed. Usually I am tense; negative things, questions, fill my mind. Will I forget the words? Will I sing out of tune? When I used the breathing technique before I sang, all the negatives left my head. They were replaced by positive thoughts. I sang better because my mind was at ease.

Catherine and my daughter, Clare, sang together in the Concordia College children's choir and I could easily recognise when they were using the meditation. They looked more confident and sang more strongly. Whenever they forgot to use the technique, they were more easily distracted and less in control.

## Perfect Shot

> I at any rate know that it is not 'I' who must be given credit for this shot. 'It' shot and 'It' made the hit.[5]

Several decades ago, a German professor of philosophy, Eugen Herrigel, wrote a very special book describing his experiences while learning archery (*Kyudo*) in Japan. The study of *Kyudo* was not regarded as a sport but as a long and arduous spiritual journey during which a person learnt to lose the self and, by this loss, to perfect 'the self'. After many years, he learnt that by not concentrating on the target – by overcoming his desperation to attain his goal – he could manage to achieve an 'aimless-aim'. To help rid himself of the need to hit the centre of the target, he practised shooting his arrows while blindfolded. In this way he was able to sense the 'perfect shot'. The same approach can be used in music. I remember, years ago, my own grandmother, who continued playing the piano into her late eighties, described to me how, as a young pianist in the course of her studies, she would often play for hours in the darkness so as to increase her feeling for the music. This, she explained, enabled her to master some of the more difficult pieces. As a child, struggling with my own piano practice, I was amazed that she should have deliberately practised for such long periods in the dark. I now wished I had discussed the matter more intently with her so that I might have obtained from her a greater insight into the value of her techniques. What I did sense so strongly, however, was her love of music; it was that special passion that is such an integral part of all good performances in every aspect of life. Thomas Jefferson, the third president of the United States, once wrote in a letter to a friend: 'Music is the favourite passion of my soul.' Despite his heavy level of responsibility and duties, Jefferson's love of music ensured that he did not neglect the development of his considerable artistic talents. This is the love of music I have seen in many of the musicians and students I have worked with over the years. Only too often, however, this wonderful artistic spirit does not readily emerge – unable to express itself in a flow of perfection because it cannot free itself from the shackles of the artist's mind.

## Preparation Methods

> I arrived at a stage where I touched the music of the spheres. Then every soul became for me a music note, and all life became music.
>
> HAZRAT INAYAT KHAN[6]

One night, in Dublin, I went to a concert given by the internationally acclaimed young Japanese pianist, Noriko Ogawa. She captivated the audience with her personality and talent as she comfortably chatted between pieces. At the start of the second half of her performance, she explained how she would now have to concentrate harder as the music would be more serious. As she began to play an exquisite piece by Schumann, the atmosphere in the hall changed. There was silence as the squeaky metal chairs stopped creaking – the audience seemed scarcely to be breathing. It was as if the pianist had become a magnet attracting our energy, drawing us into her perfection of action.

After the performance, Mr Abe of the Japanese Embassy arranged for me to have a short interview with Noriko Ogawa about her methods of preparation. She answered graciously as a stream of well-wishers passed by, explaining how she didn't make use of any formal preparation methods: 'I am affected by the music – it just happens. The music does it for me.' Noriko seems to be one of the fortunate few who naturally concentrate on the task in hand and tune readily into the 'zone'; she performs effortlessly, as though her years of training were all so easy.

As I watched and listened, I recalled scenes of the renowned basketball player, Michael Jordan, dancing and gliding through the air with apparent ease. The Chicago Bulls coach, Phil Jackson – who in fact uses Christian Zen philosophy in training his team – describes in his book[7] how Jordan was not too interested in using these methods because he felt he didn't need them. Phil Jackson agreed that in fact this was probably an accurate enough assessment. There are indeed a rare few of the many gifted athletes and musicians who can consistently and naturally tune into the 'zone'.

The ability to enter the 'zone' readily is perhaps the factor that makes the difference between top international performers and competitors – as Irish Olympic sailing coach Trevor Millar suggested to me several years ago:

> I always felt that as a coach, you could help a competitor develop only so far. I now think that the key to the missing ten percent can be obtained by using a Zen approach.[8]

With the use of a meditation programme, musicians and singers who find it difficult to achieve a state of relaxed concentration consistently can now tune into this state when necessary. Feeling in control of distractions, they are able to ensure that they can at last achieve their full potential in their music.

## Playing in Harmony

The music teacher in the public school in the Bronx where I was working, Charles Kolataze, was full of enthusiasm about the meditation programme I was using with the students. He himself had used breathing techniques with his classes of flute players over the years but had found it difficult to motivate the children to breathe in the correct way. Now that the children were incorporating meditation into their school work, we discussed how it might be easier for him to begin to use these techniques in his music lessons again. The following day, I listened to the children practising and preparing for a concert. As a group, they were not playing in harmony; indeed, they sounded somewhat breathless. It may have all come together on the actual day – it often does as we all know – but the unpredictability can be somewhat stressful. On the day of the concert, Charles decided to seek some extra help. Just before the performance was to commence, he told the group to breathe gently together and to concentrate on an imaginary feather (see Chapter 6) – as they had been doing in class. With their energy harnessed, their flutes seemed to play in unison for the first time and their performance was much better than expected.

The young pianist and singer, nine-year-old Narelia, had also experienced problems in rehearsal the previous day. At the concert, however, she played strongly and maintained a focused performance. She told me afterwards how she used the meditation for her singing:

> I was practising one of the songs for the concert this morning. I sang the song once and I noticed the words stuck in my throat. I had doubts. I straightened my back, breathed and calmed down. The breathing helped me.

Narelia had also realised how important her posture was to ensure the correct breathing and she had automatically straightened her back.

Recently, three of the most creative teachers at this school in the Bronx have combined their talent to create a modern version of the musical 'Hello Dolly'. Lorraine Conforte, whose speciality is drama and dance, has been using meditation in her work for some time. She also worked enthusiastically with my techniques and her classes were some of the most receptive to the ideas in the whole school. The children also showed great improvement in their studies and exam results. Lorraine, together with Mark and Charles (the art and music teachers), worked to use the breathing exercises in the preparation of this musical production in order to help the children concentrate on the task in hand, rather than on themselves.

## Royal Irish Academy of Music

On my return to Ireland, I met Dr John O'Conor, the country's best-known pianist. John is also the director of the Royal Irish Academy of Music in Dublin, and we discussed how the Zen meditation techniques might be beneficial to his students. Subsequently, I gave a series of workshops at the Academy and found the students there to be extremely receptive to the techniques.

## Perception of the Audience

Several music students have told me that the audience is a major factor in distracting them from focusing on their performance. One talented pianist, Finghin, said: 'Certain people in the audience make me feel nervous.' Another two students, Anne and Suzanne, believed that they were subject to feelings of 'paranoia' with respect to the audience. Accordingly, instead of concentrating on the task in hand – their music – the students found themselves distracted by the audience. This, of course, is not restricted to music students, it is also a problem commonly experienced by many teachers, lecturers and others involved in public speaking or performing. For a performer who is not relaxed or focused, the audience can be a distracting influence; any movement, even scratching of the head or yawning, may be viewed as an overt signal of boredom or criticism. When the performer is in the 'flow state', however, the members of the audience are observed but no attention is paid to them.

## Stress Symptoms

My heart was beating so fast that I couldn't even breathe.

Some of the students reported that they experienced physical symptoms of stress, such as increased heart rate, poor breathing and a great deal of tension in the centre of their backs. Robin, whose discipline was singing, found that he was calm enough while walking out onto the stage; however, during his performance his shoulders would start to rise as he became more tense – his attempts at relaxation had little effect. Maria felt that for her the worst scenario was when '... panic led to muscular tension and technical failure'; even on less stressful occasions she found that: 'Feeling nervous inhibits my performances technically and musically.' A very good musician, she readily admitted that her 'flow of expression' was being held back somewhat by her degree of nervous tension.

## Pre-Performance Nerves

The symptoms arising from pre-performance nerves often prove to be a major negative factor for many students. Parallels can be seen in the lead-up to an important exam or to a sports competition. Sometimes, the occurrence of a delay can be devastating for an athlete or a student. The energy which should be harnessed, ready for the race or the exam, is often dissipated into anxiety symptoms. If some method of coping with such anxiety is not used, the performance can be greatly undermined or diminished even before the musician reaches the stage. I have encountered many students, in fact, who felt that the fear of knowing they were likely to be nervous actually increased their anxiety levels. At this stage they had developed a 'fear of fear' – anticipation of anxiety made them worse.

## Present Moment

> Not the past; and not the future,
> but the precious present.[9]

Concentrating on the music and staying in the present moment is a problem for many musicians. They are often distracted by their last performance or the previous piece of music. I met one musician, Sarah, who felt she was '... concentrating too much on the wrong things'. Her main distractions were a sense of self-doubt and the lack of an adequate belief in herself. Another performer, Suzanne, was afraid of making a mistake in her music; while yet another, Ann, felt that when she was playing the flute, she concentrated more on the worry of getting through the piece than on the music itself. Consequently, all of them felt that their concentration on the actual music was deficient.

## Self-doubts

For most performers self-doubt is, of course, a major problem. Many of the students that I worked with had tried to devise coping methods to deal with this serious distraction. For example one student, Tara, had tried to think positively about her performance: 'I try not to think about the hard passages. A couple of bars before those passages I think to myself I can do it – but there is always some doubt in my mind.' Even though Tara tried hard to be positive she could not eliminate all the doubts by positive thinking alone. This is because nothing had really changed; telling ourselves that we can do a task may help, but it doesn't solve the problem totally. There is no reason to believe that, on a given occasion, we can concentrate and perform perfectly when in fact perfect performance has only rarely occurred previously. The method of meditation is a much more tangible technique of control than the use of verbal affirmations. At the very least, it can produce a relaxed physiological state – lowered heart and respiration rates. At best, it can also help the student to tune into the 'flow state' – into a state of perfection, or peak performance.

## Silent Centre of Quiet

Several of the students had rarely or never achieved the 'flow state'. They could not recall being in that perfect state of mind when everything went right, when they experienced total harmony with their music. This meant that they had rarely been in a state without distraction while performing – a state where they could concentrate solely on their music. For these students, much of their time was taken up with self-doubts, with worries about the audience or about their own performance. Their energy was dissipated into irrelevant distractions – rather than being harnessed and tuned into their 'silent centre of quiet'.

The distractionless state of being in the 'silent centre of quiet', however, was achieved almost every day during practice by one student, Maria. She found, nevertheless, that although in performances she could achieve a form of intense concentration – where she focused on every single note – this only happened with pieces of music that she felt she had fully mastered technically. Even in these cases, she sometimes experienced lapses in concentration. In performances, a perfect state of 'mindfulness' continued to elude her. Maria described this state as: '... total relaxation, mentally and physically; it feels like I can play almost anything – the music flows.'

One singer, Robin, had achieved this perfect performance only on one occasion that he could identify readily: 'I remember every detail. After the first song I stopped to think and realised how well I had sung and then it was gone. The second song was not so good.' Once we become conscious of how well we are doing – as soon as we are aware of this state of perfect concentration – then we lose it. Another student, Tara, also experienced this state occasionally, in practice, when: 'I am totally unaware of everything around me and I find myself as if I'm waking up.'

## Readjusting their Attitude

All of the students from the Royal Irish Academy of Music took the concept of 'peak performance' very seriously. Even those who initially found the meditation difficult were able to gain some advantage by readjusting their attitude to exams and musical performances. They began to concentrate on their music rather than allow their energy to be dissipated into thoughts of success or failure.

In the past, Anne had believed that the only way to be successful was '... to beat everyone else'. As a result of being introduced to the concepts of the 'Peak Performance' programme, she realised that she was her own rival. Viewed in this light, any thoughts of competing against her fellow musicians were really only distractions that prevented her from achieving her own best performance. She remarked how

'... over the week I've really thought about achieving the best I can. This has made me feel more relaxed and better about myself.'

These ideas were shared by Finghin who found: 'I was concentrating on fulfilling my potential and doing the best I could.' As a result, he felt that his '... piano practice was more focused'.

## Efficient Use of Time

After starting to use the 'Peak Performance' technique, some students found that they were using their time more efficiently. For example Tara, who plays the cello, found that the meditation helped her to stop 'panicking' about the amount of work she had to complete: 'I was able to achieve more results in a shorter space of time, without as much practising as I would have had to do before.' As Tara realised, so much of our time and energy is directed into worrying about our commitments and workload, rather than simply doing what we have to do to accomplish things.

Violinist Sarah found the meditation useful for yet another reason. Practising sometimes proved difficult for her because she often got very claustrophobic when she walked into a room and closed the door behind her. At one practice session she began to meditate for about a minute, while standing at the door of the practice room. When she had finished the meditation, 'the room seemed bigger and I wasn't worried about being hemmed in on all sides'. Sarah found her violin practice was much improved on that occasion. All of these results have implications in the area of health and stress-related disorders and we had some interesting discussions on these subjects.

## Refocusing

The musicians wondered if they could use the meditation to refocus and trigger the 'zone' during their actual performance, rather than just at break periods. The singers in particular felt that bursts of meditation would interfere with their own breathing patterns.

However, Robin came up with an interesting possible solution to this problem. He was rehearsing his various songs for a competition, when he was joined by another renowned singer, who asked him to sing. Robin began to sing but the first line of the song '... went very badly'. Before he began to sing the second line, he visualised the class practising meditation together: 'I knew that I had to get rid of her [the other singer], as a distraction.' He began to sing the second line and it went very well. 'My breath control was very good and this showed, as the singer complimented me on my breathing.'

Obviously Robin's breathing, during the first line of his song, was not very effective. By the start of the second line, however, Robin had tuned into the 'flow state' and his breathing had improved. It seems possible that the picture of all of us meditating had unconsciously triggered some diaphragmatic breathing (for him this was associated with the meditation) although consciously he had not been aware of a change in breathing. I started to develop this concept as a technique which I practised with some of the students. During a performance, the students began to learn to concentrate on the *hara* (a Japanese word meaning the lower abdomen) which could then trigger the correct breathing and consequently the 'flow state' without any conscious decision. This is the method I myself use when losing the 'flow state' at any time in public speaking.

## The Art of Irish Dancing

### 'Effortless Effort'

On several occasions, when I gave talks to some of the girls and parents at Margaret Pike's Irish Dancing School in Yonkers, New York, I encountered similarities between the experiences of the girls that I met at the school and those of some of the Olympic athletes with whom I have worked. The girls described their feelings when they naturally tuned into the 'zone'. One dancer, Tishi, felt so clearly that these occasions were special that she had no sense of self-doubt. 'I knew I would do well,' she explained. In the same way, the Olympic boxing silver medalist, Wayne McCullough from Belfast, knew every morning, when travelling into the boxing stadium at Barcelona, that he was going to perform to the best of his ability and talent. He explained to me how he was feeling like dynamite – ready to explode: 'My stomach felt like a ball of fire-power.' He felt that all of his physical and psychic energy (*ki*) was concentrated into a power that was about to explode into action.

Another of the dancers, Shannon, also felt that 'when in that state, you're effortless, you're a queen'. This is the very same 'effortless effort' experienced by top athletes. 'Peak Performance', when it occurs, looks and feels really easy, belying the years of hard work and training that are invariably required for a person to achieve the top results.

## New Costumes

> But if you are truly concentrated and have no object in mind, you may be able to create something beautiful.
>
> TAISEN DESHIMARU[10]

All of the girls at Margaret Pike's Irish Dancing School felt that a new dress was often an important factor in achieving success in competition and suggested that: 'When you get a new costume, you dance perfectly.' One of them, Jamie, said, 'When I got my new costume I was flying, jumping high – not a feeling I get often.' Ten-year-old Bridget, when she wore a new dancing dress, also felt she was moving effortlessly – she felt light, not weighed down or clumsy. This observation was acknowledged by some of the parents also who noticed a change in deportment and confidence in their daughters when they tried on their new dancing clothes. All of the girls agreed that it was not easy to get into the 'zone'; this calm, detached state of mind was not a feeling that occurred for them very frequently. On most occasions, rather than letting go of tension – transcending the self and 'flowing' into the correct moves and steps – they tensed up and hesitated. As Jamie admitted ruefully: 'In my set piece I became unnerved about doing well and I freaked out – I was concentrating on previous mistakes.' Obviously parents cannot replace these elaborate costumes very often. It is necessary, therefore, to find a less expensive and longer-lasting method of entering the 'zone'.

## Lapses in Concentration

I explained to the dancing students how an adapted form of Zen meditation might help them. I deliberately kept the explanations very simple as there was a large cross-section of ages in the class. However, even the youngest of the girls seemed to comprehend the connection between improved dancing skills and a calm focused state of mind. Times when lapses in concentration could be expected were identified: before a competition, after a mistake, or during a pause in the dancing. While practising the meditation, one girl found that new steps could be learned more easily. Instead of the new sequence seeming very complicated, the steps flowed more easily as her feet were forgotten.

Eleven-year-old Katie was selected for the Irish Dancing World Championships, held in Galway in 1996. She excelled in the finals. She was so happy when, for the first half of the contest, she performed as well as she could. Unfortunately, at some stage she became distracted and lost the 'flow state'; subsequently she forgot to meditate. Katie's experience illustrates just how important it is to keep concentrating by using short bursts of meditation during any break period so that, at all stages, it is possible to maintain a high level of concentration. When everything is going well, it is often easy to forget to do this. Wayne McCullough realised this factor and used the meditation throughout his fights: '... because it is necessary to keep that level of concentration for nine full minutes'.

Very often, it is helpful if the meditation is also used in other areas of life. Several of the young dancers used the meditation to help them during their tests in school. Jamie told me how she used the ideas when doing the New York State tests: '... and I did really well'. Katie also used the techniques '... to help me calm down' during her school exams. These girls became more motivated by seeing how the meditation programme gave them a greater feeling of control in various different situations.

## The Art of Ballet

> Indian traditional music and dance are a form of meditation.
>
> NANDINI

'One with the Dance'

I have had many interesting discussions over the years with Nandini, the wife of an Indian diplomat who was posted to Dublin. Calm and graceful, she had studied Indian music and dancing when she was younger and felt that losing one's self in the dance – becoming 'one with the dance' – produced a meditative state. Indian music and dance were, for her, a spiritual experience, not just entertainment – for a brief time, dancer and audience embark on a journey of transcendence. Another art form, where the concept of 'flow' is of great importance and turns dance into a meditative state, is ballet. Here we see the effortless ease of the dancers demonstrated as they move together in timeless harmony. After a really fine performance, the audience too can be caught up with the profound state of perfection displayed by the dancers. It is difficult to know where the performance ends and the audience begins. A ballet teacher at a school in Inchicore in Dublin, Marian Lennon, describes her own views on the 'flow state':

> I know that dance takes years of training to reach a state where the body moves easily without the appearance of great effort; but even when you have reached this high standard in your training, other internal and external influences can affect one's performance. For example, you might be unduly worried about a step and this can cause the body to tense which will inhibit the flow of energy to your muscles and joints, resulting in poor performance.

Marian remembered her own performances on stage and knew that:

> The best performances happen when you leave your own persona in the wings or outside the examination room and you become one with the dance. This is what makes a truly wonderful performer because you become one with the steps and the character you have at that moment in time.

The state that Marian was describing is a state of relaxed, heightened awareness – the 'zone' or 'flow state'. When I went to see her students, they all had felt the excitement of that state of self-transcendence; however, they all admitted that the state did not occur for them with any great frequency.

## Totally Detached

One student, Christine, described how she felt when the 'zone' occurred naturally for her one day when she was preparing for an exam:

> I felt myself aware of the people and the situation surrounding me but at the same time I felt totally detached and in control – exactly like as if I had found that inner place. I went into the exam as if I was in a different world but I knew exactly what I had to do and no one was going to break my concentration.

Christine tried to use the meditation to improve her mental state but she had found it difficult to achieve the level she had experienced on that previous occasion. She described one reason why it was not working so well:

> I don't think it worked very well (for my oral practical exam) though because there were so many distractions and I was also trying to remember the work I had to learn for the exam.

Christine highlighted a mistake that many individuals make. She thought she was meditating correctly but in fact she was concentrating on the work she needed to remember. Christine was not meditating but was focusing instead on a distraction – trying to remember everything for the exam. In order to produce a clear focused mind which allows the individual to retrieve previously memorised material, it is important to be able to meditate properly. This appears to be very simple in theory, but in practice it can be very difficult to achieve. Christine nevertheless continued to attempt to master the meditation:

> If I am worried about doing pirouettes or a développé, or if I am trying to concentrate and work hard on something in particular, I take a few deep slow breaths and try to calm myself. I can feel that it does something to help me but I still have not mastered the technique.

I met Christine again to help her with her meditation. She was very focused and calm on the day and passed her exam. The psychological side is only an adjunct to talent, good teaching and hard work. If, however, the individual is distracted or upset, the learned skill does not show itself adequately.

## Harness Energy

All of these students are very talented musicians and dancers, although some of them have only rarely been in the 'zone'. It is, in fact, very rare for any performer to achieve the 'zone' constantly, or indeed, frequently. Even top Olympic athletes, who have won many medals, have explained to me how they may only have experienced this true 'flowing' state of mind three or four times in their careers. The implication for these young students is that if they can learn to meditate correctly, then they can transcend 'the self'. They will thus be able to harness their energy and tune into this state at will and consistently begin to achieve peak performance.

# PART IV

## Motivation for Life

Maria

I was breathing and when I Stop. I didin't Know a teacher came in the class. On the test there was one hard Storie that was the one about digging, and finding. but I Start to breath and I start to fill in the questing because I remeber what Spellmin and the other lady said. The other Stories and poems was easy. I use the breathing two time. I felt Proud and happy of me after the Test. I did All of it And I tried my best.

# CHAPTER 6

# Fulfilling Potential through Meditation

## 'Peak Performance' Training Programme

### Mindfulness

> The power of mindfulness and concentration is the spiritual force behind all of the great men and women of human history.
>
> THICH NHAT HANH[1]

In this state of mindfulness, referred to by Vietnamese Zen monk Thich Nhat Hanh, the body is relaxed, the mind is alert, tuned into everything but clinging onto nothing – it is, in fact, a perfect state of body and mind. This is a state of 'peak performance' where, emptied of distractions of fame or gain, at one with paintbrush or pen, we let go of our ego and enable perfection of action to flow. In the martial arts and in western sport, as well as in creative and scientific areas of discovery, there are many examples of the value of this state. Stories abound of the intuitive powers of famous Japanese swordsmen in previous centuries who were able to sense and intercept potential blows from unseen attackers. These skills were not due to miraculous powers of clairvoyance; rather, they showed a highly developed state of awareness and concentration on the part of the individual swordsman.

In previous centuries, the Japanese martial arts were a matter of life and death; a lapse in concentration did not just entail the loss of a medal but meant instant death. The ancient masters suggested that the human body was more stable on the exhalation of the breath and less stable on the inhalation. Accordingly, the martial artist held that it was necessary to attack one's opponent while breathing out, and while the opponent was breathing in, so that one's strength and stability could be maximised. Such a complicated series of actions clearly cannot be worked out on a rational basis and can only be achieved in a state of relaxed concentration. This is the state in which we do our best work.

## Heightened Awareness

A few years ago, the Irish world rowing champion, Niall O'Toole, described to me how he was so in tune with his surroundings at one important race, that he sensed a rival competitor had missed a stroke. At this point Niall picked up speed and won the race. This incredible mental feat was achieved despite the combination of mental stress, physical strain and the noise of churning water at the start of an important international race. Niall, at this time, was using the adapted Zen meditation programme to help him tune into the 'zone' or 'flow state'. By doing so, he was able to attend to relevant stimuli while screening out any irrelevant interference and distraction and was thus able to gain an advantage over his opponents.

This ability to attain a heightened awareness and 'peak performance' is possible in all aspects of life. One very successful Irish dress designer, Helen McAlinden of Ramsay, told me how, when this state naturally occurred, she was able to match her designs perfectly, and instantly, with the correct fabric. Intuitively, she was able to find the correct combination of colour and texture. She began to practice Zen meditation to help her to achieve this state on a more regular basis. Writers talk of being in a trance, wondering where the words they wrote so easily could have come from. Musicians, too, talk of being in total harmony with their musical instruments. One young child, Carmela, described how she felt, as a consequence of meditating before a piano lesson:

> It felt like I wasn't playing the piano. My fingers were playing by themselves. I wasn't worried if I hit a wrong note. I was relaxed.

In this intense state, no conscious effort appears to be needed – the actions occur by themselves. To describe this verbally is very difficult and, for many years, the athletes I worked with told me they were afraid to discuss these concepts in case they sounded a little strange. Swimmers sometimes felt an out-of-body experience as they looked down on their body cutting through the water; archers sometimes saw the target expanding.

## Rigorous Discipline

Over the years, in order to help people to achieve this heightened mental state more frequently, I have been using a form of Zen meditation training which fits more easily into a Western setting. Recently, I have simplified this even further for use with young children. True Zen is, in fact, a very rigorous discipline and even many adults would rarely be prepared to put in the time and effort necessary for the full training. I have found, however, that this adapted form of Zen training is a very effective way of attaining spiritual enhancement and successful living. On a practical level, the power that can come from gently breathing and harnessing our energy in a distractionless state of mind is amazing.

> In *zazen** the body is motionless, but *ki* becomes strong through breathing.
>
> TAISEN DESHIMARU[2]

In this context, I recall a long and insightful discussion I had one day with Park Jong-Soon, from the Korean Embassy, about the significance of meditation in the Korean culture. He emphasised the central rôle of breathing in Korean tradition. He explained how he himself found meditation to be a potent mechanism for harnessing *ki* (universal energy) in order to concentrate the mind. He felt meditation could also be utilised for healing physical illnesses – an idea I myself have used with some success over the years.

## Habituation of Brain Waves

When I was in Japan many years ago, Professor William Johnston introduced me to the work of Professor Tomio Hirai who, for several decades, conducted scientific research into the brain waves emitted during Zen meditation. He suggested

* The practice of sitting meditation.

that whether or not one actually believes in the religious or philosophical concepts of Zen is largely irrelevant. As he pointed out, individuals can use '... the scientific aspects of the techniques of Zen meditation to bring about changes in the awareness and thus find mental stability and harmony'.[3] His findings suggest that, in Zen meditation, a state is achieved in which the brain functions at an optimal level of performance. The brain and body are deeply relaxed but, despite this, the brain waves in trained Zen monks respond continuously to stimuli. In one series of experiments, Hirai found that if a simple click – or audio-stimulus – was repeated many times at a fixed interval to individuals with no experience of Zen meditation who were sitting with their eyes closed, habituation occurred as the individual became used to the audio-stimulation. On the other hand, Zen monks – with their eyes open – continued to respond to each new click, regardless of the length of time the stimuli continued.

In this research, the Zen monks appeared to react to all occurrences of stimuli as if they were fresh and new – despite the fact that such 'distractions' had been repeated over a long period of time. The control group, on the other hand, began to habituate after about five to seven 'clicks'. This state of heightened awareness, or optimal performance of the brain found in Zen meditation, is necessary for us to achieve 'peak performance' in all areas of life – each stimulus is attended to and then let go. This becomes the process of tuning into relevant stimuli yet cutting out irrelevant distractions – the state of mind that is essential for excellence. It was such findings that helped to trigger my own interest in this area of research. Shortly afterwards, I incorporated this thinking into my own techniques which I used when working with Irish athletes on their preparations for the Moscow Olympic Games.

# The Learning Zone

## Training Programme to Achieve a State of Relaxed Concentration

The following programme is a very effective way to tune into the state of optimal performance – a perfect combination of relaxation and concentration.

> Your breath should be light, even, and flowing, like a thin stream of water running through the sand.
>
> THICH NHAT HANH[4]

### Simple Relaxation

Loosen tight belts and clothing and sit on a chair. Inhale gently through the nose, clenching every muscle group simultaneously. Bend down and clasp the hands around the knees, tighten up the facial and body muscles and experience the tension in all the muscles. Slowly let go of the tension, releasing hands and exhaling gently, relax back against the chair, let your feet flop out sideways. The eyes should be gently closed, not tightly clenched, and there should be a small gap between the centre of the lips.

Quietly breathing from the diaphragm, visualise the ocean. Breathe through the nose. Imagine the colours of blue, green, cool, refreshing waves lapping against the seashore. Concentrate on the waves for a few minutes.

Now gently move your body, then stretch your arms and legs and slowly open your eyes. You will feel relaxed and revitalised.

# Zen Meditation Programme – Adapted for College Students and Other Adults.

## Correct Position for Meditation

- The most effective position for Zen meditation is the lotus or half-lotus position. As, however, this programme is adapted to fit into a Western culture, I have found it preferable to use an ordinary chair.
- Choose a quiet room, at least when you are starting to meditate. (Later on you will be able to cope with increasing levels of distraction.) Sit on a chair without leaning against the back, feet squarely on the ground, hands flat, palm-down on thighs just above the knees – back straight, head straight, with eyes looking down a metre or so ahead. Use a chair of the correct height if possible. It is better not to sit on a patterned carpet which may prove too distracting. Wear loose clothing and do not look at a watch – that is a distraction. Do not stare at a spot or pattern; let your gaze be diffused – you are focusing internally, not externally. If you feel anything strange, just stop meditating – you are perhaps hyperventilating, straining your breathing or staring fixedly at something. Any 'visual distortions' (*Makyo*) are definitely not to be encouraged! When you have finished, move your body around loosely and stand up slowly. At the beginning you can set an alarm or ask someone to tell you when the time has passed. Soon you will be able to gauge this for yourself.

## How to Breathe

- Inhale deeply from the diaphragm through the nose, exhale through the nostrils, the exhalation being naturally a little longer than the inhalation. Breathe deeply but do not strain; do not raise your shoulders as you are breathing, keep your shoulders relaxed. If you have difficulty breathing through your nose for any reason, close your mouth in a relaxed position – lips closed with a tiny gap in the centre – this should aid your nasal breathing. In order to breathe correctly, keep your back straight and maintain good posture throughout the exercise.

### How to Deal with Distractions

- When you are faced with a distraction (as you frequently will be) learn to acknowledge it, to look at it and let it go. Do not push the thought away, do not cling to it – quietly let it go and then gently bring your mind back to the stage on which you were concentrating before you were distracted. Eventually, thoughts will pass in and out of your mind, not attended to – just there, like fleeting impressions on a mirror.

## Adapted Stages of a Graduated Zen Meditation Programme

### Stage One:

- **Feather**. Imagine you have a tiny down feather on the end of your nose and as you exhale, do so as gently as possible so that the feather is not dislodged. Concentrate only on the feather.

### Stage Two

- **Rhythm**. As you inhale, say to yourself 'I shall breathe in.' As you exhale, say 'I shall breathe out.' This should produce a gentle rhythm on which you concentrate.

### Stage Three

- ***Hara***. Breathe in through the nose and, when the lungs have expanded, mentally push the breath down into the lower abdomen or *hara* (of course, the breath is gradually escaping all the time through the nostrils). Concentrate on the internal action of pushing down.

In my earlier sports programme, I used many more stages of meditation, taken from a variety of sources[5,6] and developed from my own experience over the years. I have found, however, all of the stages outlined above to be particularly effective in the areas of education and creativity. Choose and practise each one of these stages – stage three appears to bring about the state of deepest concentration. It is preferable, therefore, to use this as a final stage.

## Study and Exam Programme for College Students and Adults

### 1. Home Training Programme (Every day)

- Every morning meditate for five minutes before breakfast. If the morning is not a convenient time choose any time during the day – but not after a heavy meal.
- At the beginning, when you are still learning to meditate, choose a quiet place to practice – eventually you will be able to meditate effectively anywhere.
- Practice short bursts of meditation – two or three breaths – throughout the day, before telephone calls, in the bus or train, or while walking along the street.

- Remember that you are not simply breathing but rather concentrating on one of the three stages of meditation mentioned above.

## 2. Study Programme

- Sit at your desk, clear a space in front of you and gently meditate for two or three minutes before starting your study.
- During study or homework, practise bursts of breathing every now and again to remain focused. This is especially necessary if you feel tired, bored or you are losing concentration for any reason.
- Meditate before beginning each new subject.

## 3. Class Programme

- Before the start of class meditate for a minute or two.
- To keep focused throughout the class period, practise bursts of meditation. (This is particularly useful whenever you feel tired or your concentration is beginning to lapse.)

## 4. Exam Programme

- A student's approach to an exam should be similar to that of an athlete preparing for a competition.
- On the morning of an exam, when you wake up, tighten up and clench all the muscles in your body and face. Then let go – relax gently and slowly let the tension out. Do this several times.
- Do five minutes' meditation before breakfast – look briefly at any distraction and then let it go.

- Every now and then, until you leave the house, continue short bursts of meditation – two or three breaths. Do this when you feel worried. Worry is a distraction, let it go.
- In the car or on the bus, do short bursts of meditation now and again to keep focused, relaxed, and to rid yourself of distractions.
- In college, sitting at your desk, take another two or three breaths. Don't try to remember all you know – just concentrate on the stage of meditation you have chosen.
- When your test paper is placed in front of you, gently meditate. Feel calm, relaxed and focused. Remember that feelings of panic are a distraction!
- Open the test booklet when you are told – turn to the correct page and take another short burst of meditation – start the exam. Remember your energy must be directed onto your exam, not distractions.

## Breathing Programme – Adapted for Children aged 8-14 years

Adults supervising children can use the following instructions. Try to ensure that the breathing is quiet, comfortable and not strained.

### 1. Correct Position for Meditation

- Sit up straight in your chair, hands on knees or on your desk, feet squarely on the ground.
- Do not hold your shoulders in a rigid position – lower them. Close your eyes.

- Breathe gently through the nose, breathe from the stomach; do not move the chest and shoulders.
- Do not strain your breathing, do not raise your shoulders or move your chest.
- Keep your eyes closed if you prefer.
- Imagine you have a tiny feather on the end of your nose. As you breathe out through your nose do so as gently as possible so that the feather is not blown away.
- Focus only on the feather.
- Breathe in and out for two to three or four to five breaths (preferably no more than five inhalations and exhalations for young children although some older children in this group will feel happy with several more – ten or twelve perhaps).

### 2. How to Deal with Distractions

- Distraction – when you think of a distraction look at it, let it go, and bring your mind back to the feather. Remember, there are many kinds of distractions – noises, other children's voices, worry, feeling ill, thoughts of self-doubt.

## Study and Exam Programme for Students aged 8-14 years

### 1. Home Training Programme (Every day)

- Every morning, practise the breathing before breakfast. Do this for several breaths (no more than five) and concentrate only on the feather.
- Practise short bursts of breathing, one or two breaths, every now and again during the day.

## 2. Study Programme

- Sit at your desk, clear a space in front of you, breathe for two or three breaths, and concentrate on the feather.
- Start your study or homework.
- If you start to feel tired, or your concentration begins to lapse, carry out a short burst of breathing to help you to refocus.

## 3. Class Programme

- Before the beginning of each class practise one or two breaths. Concentrate on the feather.
- If you feel you are not concentrating properly, carry out one or two breaths from time to time.

## 4. Exam Programme

- Get a good night's sleep the night before an exam – if you begin to think of the test at night and can't sleep, do some relaxation or a little gentle breathing. Concentrate on the feather.
- In the morning, when you wake up, tighten up and clench all the muscles in your body. Then let go; relax gently – slowly let the tension out.
- Take two or three breaths while concentrating on the feather – look briefly at any distraction that occurs and then let it go.
- Every now and then – until you leave the house – continue to take two or three breaths gently, and concentrate on the feather. Do this, especially when you feel worried. Worry is a distraction, let it go.

- In the car, train, or on the bus, take two or three breaths every few minutes to keep focused and relaxed; this will help you to rid yourself of distractions.
- In school, when sitting at your desk, take another two or three breaths. Don't try to remember all you know – just concentrate on the feather.
- When your test paper is placed in front of you in the exam, breathe gently while concentrating on the feather. Keep calm, relaxed and focused. Remember that feelings of panic are a distraction!
- Open the test booklet when you are told – turn to the correct page and take another two breaths concentrating on the feather – then begin the test. Remember your energy must be directed on your exam paper, not on distractions.

## How to Focus when Answering Questions

- Maths – breathe and concentrate on the feather before you begin to attempt each problem. REMEMBER TO BREATHE BEFORE EVERY PROBLEM, NOT JUST THE DIFFICULT ONES!
- Reading Comprehension – breathe and concentrate on the feather. GET AN OVERVIEW OF THE MEANING OF EACH SENTENCE. Breathe at the end of the paragraph – get an overview of the meaning of the paragraph to make sure you understand it. Continue to the end of the section. Breathe and concentrate on the feather before answering each of the questions.
- Writing – breathe and concentrate on the feather before starting to write. Breathe again if you find that you have lost your concentration.

## Breathing and Study Programme – Adapted for Young Children aged 5-7

Adults who are supervising this agegroup can use the following instructions. Try to ensure that the breathing is comfortable, not strained.

> It's a good feeling.
>
> SIX-YEAR-OLD STUDENT'S COMMENT, NEW YORK

### 1. Correct Position for Breathing

- Sit up straight in your chair, with hands on your knees or desk. Close your eyes, and breathe gently through the nose from the stomach, do not move your chest and shoulders. Imagine you have placed a snowball on top of your head, you are nice and warm and the ice crystals are slowly starting to run down your face and head. You are feeling cool and calm. Concentrate on the ice crystals sliding down your face.
- Distractions – when you think of a distracting thought, look at the thought briefly and let it go, bring your mind back immediately to the ice crystals.

### 2. Homework Programme

- Breathe gently for one or two breaths. Think of the cool snowball. Start your homework.

### 3. Exam Programme

- Before your test, sit at your desk and take one or two breaths. Think of the snowball. If you have difficulty with any question breathe one or two breaths to calm down and refocus.

# Programme for the Creative Arts – College Students and Adults

> I sat down. Started to breathe in this special way, telling myself I've got to ignore all distractions. Fine, dandy, sure it probably won't work and I was maybe wasting my time. But when I got up, I had nothing but pure clarity and great focus in my otherwise cluttered mind. It felt really good, to feel perfect.
>
> JOHN, STUDENT
> ROYAL IRISH ACADEMY OF MUSIC

This programme should be done in conjunction with the Home Training Programme (p. 139–142). When using the following methods use the feather or snowball stages for young children; they should meditate for several breaths rather than minutes.

## Art Programme

- Meditate for several minutes before starting to draw or paint, gather up your energy gently. If you are losing concentration at any point, from tiredness, boredom or distraction, then do bursts of breathing at this point to help you refocus.

## Writing Programme

- Clear your desk. Meditate for several minutes before starting to write. If you have a loss of concentration at any point, meditate for several breaths – this will help you to trigger the 'flow state' and also to refocus. The meditation is also excellent for clearing your mind and formulating new creative ideas.

## Music Programme

**Practice**

- Before starting to play an instrument or to sing, carry out several minutes of meditation. From time to time, during the lesson or practice, carry out bursts of breathing to keep focused throughout the practice session.

**Recital**

- When you wake up in the morning, use your relaxation exercises. Then meditate for five minutes. Bursts of breathing throughout the day should become more frequent as the concert draws near. Before you start playing or performing, meditate while on the stage, then carry out bursts of meditation during any rest periods on and off the stage.

## Dance Programme

**Practice**

- Meditate for several minutes before warm-up exercises. Breathing for short bursts should be done during any rest period and prior to any new or difficult steps.

**Performance**

- When you wake up on the morning of a performance, relax for several minutes. Meditate for five minutes. Bursts of breathing, during the day, should be done with increas-ing frequency as the performance draws near. Before going on the stage meditate for several breaths. During any brief rest period throughout the performance breathe gently; if a mistake is made, re-trigger the flow by meditating.

**Effective Performance**

- In order for this programme to work effectively you must meditate correctly. The following quote, from ten-year-old student Nicola from PS 97 in New York, shows that we may not always be meditating fully, even when we think we are:

---

I used Felictys breathing and It
didn't work for me this time it
made my regular breathing harder for
me it always used to work
but not this time this test was
too hard

---

Nicola thought she was meditating correctly but, in fact, she was worrying about the difficulty of the test. It is important to keep a straight posture, to breathe correctly from the diaphragm and to concentrate fully on the stage of meditation that you are studying. Do not day-dream – look at any distractions and let them go; then return immediately to the meditation. Correct breathing and 'mindful' meditation are essential to the achievement of a state of heightened awareness – a state in which we can achieve excellence. This is an excellence which is dependent on both our ability and our preparation. If, however, we have truly done our best then we have achieved our own level of perfection. In the words of a wise Native American:

> The man who preserves his selfhood ever calm and unshaken by the storms of existence – not a leaf, as it were, astir on the tree; not a ripple upon the surface of the shining pool – this, in the mind of the unlettered sage, is the ideal attitude and conduct of life.
>
> OHIYESA (SANTEE DAKOTA), 1902[7]

# CHAPTER 7

## The Art of Motivation

### Be the Best You Can Be

> Not hammer-strokes, but dance of the water sings the pebbles into perfection.
>
> RABINDRANATH TAGORE[1]

Among the beautiful wisdom and mystical symbolism of the words written by the Bengali Nobel Laureate, Rabindranath Tagore, runs a strong thread of 'ordinary mind' that is very similar to Zen thought. Just as many centuries of the persistent gentle action of the water, not the brutal force of the hammer, brings about the perfect beauty of the shape and form of stones and pebbles; so too, the influences to which the child is exposed can have enormous effect in the shaping of their life. Gentle, loving, consistent behaviour brings about beauty and true growth, whereas force and violence can contribute to a disturbed, damaged mind and body.

## Refining Their Own Lives

This concept of gentle action as opposed to force reminds me, in a very tangible way, of the 'Hanawa' household which I visited in Yokohama many years ago. This was a place, looked after for many years by Mr and Mrs Hanawa, where boys who had caused problems and had been brought before the family court were sent. Here, in this homely but disciplined house, the boys were taught to develop both a sense of self-respect and a responsibility to society by the gentle method of a practical form of meditation. Kneeling around a long low table, the young Japanese boys polished rough stones into objects of beauty, day after day; they were, in fact, also polishing and refining their own lives.

For the boys, their entire time spent in this house was a form of 'meditation in action'. The circular movement of the soft cloth against the rough stone was similar to the gentle action of the brush against the ink-stone in *sumi-e* painting – a preparation for a composed mind. Instead of spending time in more punitive situations, they spent several months in a structured, caring, home-like environment. Here, they were treated with respect and were able to reflect on their responsibility to society, and on their future life. The meditative action of polishing the stones seemed to work by helping to calm the boys and give them more control over their behaviour. Tuning into their quiet creative centre, they were able to produce prized objects of art. These stones were unusual – under the rough exterior lay a fossil in the shape of a chrysanthemum (*kiku*). After weeks and months of polishing, the stones shone like black marble and the fossils were exposed in shades of white and grey. Many of the finished products were given as presents to various monarchs of

Europe who came to visit this house. Having spent much of their short lives involved in destruction, these boys were at last given a unique opportunity to produce works of great beauty that were considered worthy of the palaces of Europe.

In this way, the Hanawas succeeded in helping many boys to regain their self-respect, to become sufficiently motivated to cast off their old approach to life and to learn new, more appropriate, ideas and responses. The gentle, motivated approach of this couple seemed to produce results which were more impressive than those attained by the harsher methods of many institutions in other parts of the world.

## Coaching Secrets

> Leadership is a matter of intelligence, trustworthiness, humaneness, courage, and sternness.
>
> SUN TZU[2]

In sport, motivation is obviously of particular importance. I have worked with many coaches and managers, and several stand out for me as excellent motivators and instigators of team spirit – thus facilitating optimum performance. One of those is Brian Kerr, now manager of the Irish Youth football teams. When I worked with him, he was the manager of St Patrick's Athletic Football Club and his team was totally loyal and dedicated to the ideal of excellence. Down to earth, with very little sign of ego, he carried everyone along on a wave of unity and enthusiasm. It is a difficult task to get me to stand in the wind and sleet at the edge of a soccer field for the entire length of a practice session, or a full game, but Brian managed to achieve this. Such was his belief in the rôle of psychology in sport, that I felt very honoured to be asked to work with his team and to stand for hours in the freezing cold, clutching a mug of steaming tea! There was no screaming or shouting on the field, no flare-ups of bad temper or tantrums in the dressing room, just fairness, a love of the game and a willingness to involve all members of the team equally. These were the secrets of the success of Brian and his colleagues. Brian's assistant, Noel O'Reilly, also an excellent coach, sought to explain to me why he and Brian were regarded as such a good team. 'It's our ordinariness,' he suggested – I think he's right. They do their best because they love their sport. They don't try to impress, but rather see their work as an enjoyable challenge. Brian and Noel do not try to be special and – because of this – they are indeed at the top.

## New Methods

Cuban coach Nicholas Cruz, who has been working with the Irish boxing team for many years, also achieves great results with his special motivational approach. Nicholas sees the importance of team spirit and psychological techniques and he uses Oriental methods to maintain stability and calm. Another great motivator in Irish sport is swimming coach Carole Walsh. Every morning and evening Carole is at the pool, solving problems and encouraging improvement in the swimmers. She is always full of enthusiasm as she reaches out, with new methods, to every area of the swimmers' performances. Her aim is to help the swimmers to achieve their full potential at all levels; she is not just interested in working with Olympic hopefuls. Like Brian Kerr, Noel O'Reilly and Nicholas Cruz, her integrity is a major factor in her success.

Another coach with whom I worked decided that brutality was the answer – not team spirit or motivating techniques. He berated the college team members constantly and was unwilling to leave them alone with me – I soon discovered why on the one occasion he did so. The team members, instead of concentrating on the constructive elements of their own play, were only interested in explaining how harmful to their personal self-esteem and to their game the approach of their coach was. The team disintegrated before my eyes as their hidden grievances came out in a bitter and destructive way. I realised that unless this all changed, the team was – sadly – not going to be successful. The coach was unwilling to change his methods, he was more interested in his own image than in the success of the team and he truly believed his techniques would bring about improvement in their play. The more he beat them with his psychological hammer, however, the less the team improved.

## Values and Ideals

> Zen masters are often great personalities; and among the layman practising Zen we find men of strong character, great statesmen and businessmen.
>
> H.M. ENOMIYA LASSALLE SJ[3]

Motivation is of importance not only in sport, but obviously is relevant to the whole spectrum of life and particularly to education. There are many stories of young athletes and soccer players who, despite great talent and opportunities, wasted their time and energy over the years, and spent the rest of their lives full of regrets. Equally there are as many stories of adults who, as children, had no interest in school, didn't fulfil their potential and who were forced into routine, low-paid jobs for which they were not suited. It is extremely important to enable a child to see the relevance of education. Then they can be helped to work for a long-term goal which demands nightly study and their full attention every day in school. Unfortunately, it is not easy for a small child, or even a college student, to know what subjects they really like, or to which ones they are suited. At this stage in a child's education, it is important that parents and teachers provide guidance and support. One way to do this is by our living out the values and ideals we wish to impart to our children. Many parents have complained to me over the years that their children will not read or study at home. When I ask them if they – the children's closest rôle models – ever read anything themselves, they reply in horror: 'I don't have time to read, I just watch television to relax.' Example is far more effective than words can ever be. We cannot expect our children to see the purpose of activities that we so blatantly undervalue.

## Blur of Teaching Faces

As the poet Rabindranath Tagore puts it so beautifully, in the quote at the beginning of this chapter: we can't beat anything or anyone into submission or into perfection. As parents or teachers, we have to inspire and encourage. We have to show the beauty and meaning, in our own lives, of the kind of ideals we wish to pass on to our children. We have to provide stimulation at home and in school. We must show children the importance of studying today so as to gain results tomorrow.

All of us can probably remember at least one or, if we are lucky, more teachers in our lives who have played a positive part in our future careers. For me, one such teacher at my school in England was Mrs Merrick, my fourth class primary school teacher. A tiny figure, with white hair neatly curled, she seemed to me to be very old at the time but, despite this, she appeared very interesting and full of life. She was particularly interested in drama and, as well as academic subjects, she taught us to act, to improvise and to be creative. She was a memorable figure among the blur of teaching faces that I encountered. In grammar school, my Latin teacher stood out as a positive influence. She was stern, and kept strict discipline, but she had a passionate love of her subject that enabled her to bring to life the hidden wonders of Cicero and Virgil. Both of these teachers made a huge impact on my school life. They must have become bored, teaching unresponsive pupils day after day, year after year, yet they never seemed to lose interest or the sense of challenge.

Home influences are equally important. As a child, I listened to my father's account of his scientific research. He made everything sound so interesting, whether it was his scientific work at the university, his travels attending conferences all around the world or his interest in social justice and peace. At night, he would write his research papers or edit various international journals. I wasn't too excited about my own school work and I tried to get away with as much corner-cutting as I could. Watching my father's dedication, however, I was prepared to believe that there was a big world of interesting possibilities ahead that made study worthwhile. It is important to show children that delaying gratification can lead to future gains.

## Dance of the Water

Maybe teachers and parents could learn from the approach of coaches and team managers in sport. We can learn whether to go for the tactics of the hammer, smashing and crashing at the fragility of the individual, or to go for the gentle persistence of the dance of the water refining and smoothing the path to the future. Our own interest and enthusiasm can help us to encourage our children in their work and play. That has to be the choice: whether to make our job a joyful interesting experience, to see each child and each day as a worthwhile challenge – or whether to find everything a tedious and boring task.

## Disruptive Behaviour

> There was a door to which I found no key:
> There was a veil past which I could not see:
>
> OMAR KHAYYAM[4]

Some children are quite self-motivated, while other children need more help; however, all need to be treated with respect – not always an easy task, I admit. Every child needs to be seen as a unique individual with something to offer to society. Often, because teachers in today's environment are stressed and overworked, the value of the child is not seen. Positive reinforcement is generally given to the articulate student and negative attention shown to the disruptive student. The child lost in the middle is often ignored. Labelling is an easy way out of an overtaxed situation. In most overcrowded classrooms, it takes too long to work out the reason for some disruptive behaviour patterns. Sometimes, however, the child will open up to an outsider. It would be very useful – as has been done in some schools – to encourage volunteers to take on the rôle of caring, interested observers in the classroom. Maybe this would help the children to discuss, and form a solution to, some of their problems.

## The Art of Motivation

### Teachers

How to teach more effectively and to improve the motivation of the child.

'I used the tachniques [*sic*] before the test and when I got a blood test and it calmed me down.'

**Do the very best you can**

A teacher's job is probably one of the most difficult and important in society – try to do the best job you can. Do not be bored or just 'put in time' on the job. Do not spend time proving your ability to supervisors or colleagues. You are here to do a good job, not just to appear to be doing a good job. Focus on the task in hand; do not worry about other things.

Do not put pressure on the children simply to get better results for yourself.

### Parents

How to maintain motivation in the family and to work more effectively with children and teachers.

'I feel relaxed because breathing gently is very comfortable.'*

**Do the very best you can**

Parenting is the most difficult job of all – although equally it can be the most rewarding. Accept that we all do our best in many different ways – there is no single correct way. Do not try to be a 'super-parent'; very often this is done for the wrong reason – our own ego predominates rather than the good of the child. If children do not turn out as expected, this may not be a bad thing.

We can advise children but we can't force them into certain career or behaviour patterns.

### Children

How to help children to motivate themselves.

'This feather thing makes you relaxed. It helps you on tests. Kids get higher points by doing this.'*

**Do the very best you can**

Do not compare yourself with friends or other students. You are your own rival. If you are the best you can be, you have succeeded. It is 'cool' to be the best you can be. Everyone can be a winner, if they have fulfilled their own potential at that time. Only you know if you are truly performing well. You can fool others much of the time but not yourself.

*Quotes from New York schoolchildren

| Teachers | Parents | Children |
| --- | --- | --- |
| | It is important not to see children as extensions of ourselves, or feel that we may be judged by the impressions they make on others. If so, we are thinking of success and failure in ourselves not the benefit of the child. | |
| **Challenge**<br>Start to view difficult lessons or problematic situations as challenges – see these situations as learning experiences and as something to be overcome. Do not feel apprehensive or blasé about situations. See each day as a fresh start. The longer you have taught a class the more necessary it is to see the more challenging aspects of the subject. | **Challenge**<br>View situations or events as a challenge rather than a worry or a burden – the situation improves dramatically. Do not concentrate on the immediate difficulties. Try to see things in the longer term by focusing on small improvements in a given area. | **Challenge**<br>See every day as a challenge. Try to see each task as an opportunity to learn new skills. When you think a test is going to be easy, be sure to pay special attention – otherwise you may become careless. In a difficult situation use your 'secret weapon' – tune into the 'zone'. |
| **Live in the Present**<br>Keep your mind on the present task. Concentrate on teaching when in school. Concentrate on home problems when at home; do not mix the two areas of home and school. Stay focused, alert and fresh. | **Live in the Present**<br>Appreciate each day – time goes by very quickly for a child. Teach children to appreciate time; as with health, it is a most precious commodity to have. Help children not to worry about future problems – they may never happen. | **Live in the Present**<br>Do not think of previous or future lessons or problems. Keep your mind on the task in hand. In an exam, deal with one question at a time. Do not worry about the other questions on the test. |

| Teachers | Parents | Children |
| --- | --- | --- |
| | Teach children not to neglect to see the real joys of today in favour of the imagined joys of tomorrow. Enjoy the present moment – it is all we have. | |
| **Preconceptions**<br>It is important not to have preconceptions about your own work and that of your students. Assess your own strengths and weaknesses fairly. Try to encourage rather than label students. | **Preconceptions**<br>Do not label children – this may become a self-fulfilling prophecy. Look for attributes that can be admired, encourage and praise those; if we remain unbiased we will find many talents in our children. | **Preconceptions**<br>Do not decide you are 'no good' at certain subjects. Do assess your abilities realistically. If you have difficulties in any area try to do extra work in order to improve. |
| **Preparation**<br>Always be sure to prepare your lessons adequately. Keep up to date with your work. | **Preparation**<br>Try to spend time with the children willingly. Unlike other jobs, the rôle of parent requires constant preparation. | **Preparation**<br>Do your homework as well as you can. Prepare for tests ahead of time; a little regular study over the months before an exam rather than a lot the night before is more effective. |
| **Enjoy what you do**<br>This may not always be easy. If, however, you are keeping in mind all the above concepts, then you will probably enjoy much of what you do. | **Enjoy what you do**<br>The rôle of full-time parent – for most people – is very fleeting. If we remember this point we may enjoy parenting more. | **Enjoy what you do**<br>If you are doing your best, focusing on your work and seeing it as a challenge, then you will find school going well. |

## Perfecting Skills

I have put together the above 'psychological recipe' for successful living, which I have developed over two decades of working with Olympic athletes and with people from the artistic professions. This 'recipe', combined with the meditation programme, is designed to help us to be the best we possibly can be.

Perhaps one of the most important aspects of our lives to develop is the ability to become motivated enough to fulfil our true potential. If we confuse this with a desperation to win, we will only cause more problems for ourselves. As we all know only too well, if we are not interested in perfecting certain skills, we have little hope of bringing about an improvement. The concept of motivation, therefore, is crucial in life, in sport, and especially in education. The renowned karate master Kasuya *Sensei* told me, on his last trip to Ireland, how, for many years, he had concentrated on the concept of winning – beating his opponent was all that mattered. He knew that he needed to let go of this and reduce his level of desperation. However, the only advice he got from his coaches was: 'relax!' – a command that immediately made him tense up even more. At last, at the age of thirty-five, he understood that what he needed to do was fulfil his potential. At this point, the pressure to win began to diminish. He attained greater powers of concentration and, unaffected by the noise of the crowd or the sight of other competitors, he was able to sense the feeling of perfection. Since then, he has travelled all over the world training students in karate techniques.

In the education system we can use rewards and punishments – as psychologists and parents have done over the years – but these methods often result in short-term success only. Rewards or treats may be occasional welcome additions to a class but, if the teaching is going well, they are usually unnecessary. What is important is that the child – or older student – feels in control of their own ability, feels good about the way they are performing and knows that they are close to doing the best that they can. An objective measure of this is whether or not the child has achieved the 'zone' or 'flow state'.

On some occasions, it is possible to tune into the 'flow state' just by thinking of this concept. The only problem with this method of entering the 'zone' is that merely thinking of this 'flowing' state of mind may not always be enough to enter into it. Attempting to bring about this state can cause too much pressure on the individual to achieve it, and thus it is not attained. Meditation is a more effective way of tuning into the 'zone'. The physiological changes that are brought about by meditation help to ensure the necessary alert mind and relaxed body that an individual requires to achieve optimal performance.

## Positive Peer Pressure

> I would tell them it could improve your work and it could help you feel relaxed and calm. Also it could make you more focused and it will help you feel more confident in yourself.
>
> ELEVEN-YEAR-OLD STUDENT, PUBLIC SCHOOL 97
> NEW YORK

Over the years, the results of my studies with adults and older students were always very exciting. It was especially wonderful to see the eyes of the athlete, musician or artist light up as they described their experience of expanding the boundaries of excellence. What was most rewarding, however, was the work I started with young children in New York. Although many of these children came from underprivileged backgrounds, where there was little money and all sorts of family problems, most of them actively welcomed an opportunity to try out the new ideas and to become more focused. They expressed delight in doing the best they could and seemed to be very interested in devising methods to extend the ideas to other areas of their own lives. Obviously, this did not work for every child that I encountered but most of the children did manage to work well together and produced some amazing academic results. Peer pressure on these occasions worked in a positive sense as the children did not allow the few disruptive individuals among them to interrupt the sessions.

More than a thousand years after Chinese Zen masters told of the extraordinary power of meditation we still have much to learn. Maybe we should start to introduce the concept of the 'zone' or 'flow state' into the everyday school curriculum. If children were consistently able to concentrate at this level, they would then be able to take advantage of all the available resources in the school and, as a consequence, underachieving might be less of a problem.

# CHAPTER 8

# Moving towards a Creative New Beginning

## Human Potential

> At its simplest and most profound level, Zen is purely devoted to liberating the hidden potential of the human mind.
>
> THOMAS CLEARY[1]

If we wish to be fully human we must learn to fulfil our human potential. We must start to let go of our needs – our selfishness, our greed, our pettiness – to transcend the self and reach into the very depths of our silent soul. It is in this still point that we can find perfection – in this state of flowing, relaxed concentration we can be the best that we can possibly be.

To help individuals move towards this state of 'perfection of action', I have used an adapted form of Christian Zen that fits in with any culture or any era. By sitting in quiet meditation we can start to tune into the 'zone' or 'flow state'. This is the relaxed, concentrated state of mind in which we can achieve excellence. This is an excellence in which we are our own rival and as such, this is the only perfection we can guarantee. We might not win medals or prizes, because, however good we are, our competitors may be better. If, on the other hand, we have reached the peak of our own performance then we have truly become the winner. As we go through life, it is wonderful to have the gift of being able to experience this state of quiet perfection as and when we wish.

From my work over the years, I have found that it is never too early or too late to tune into this mental state. Achieving this state does not involve the pushy approach of the over-zealous parent depriving children of a carefree childhood by forcing them through a highly programmed, ambition-based curriculum. Nor does it require a reversion to the restricting quiet of the Victorian schoolroom where children are afraid to express themselves. This ideal mental state is where spontaneity, creativity, and clarity of thought can be tapped – it is where we encounter the silence of the soul and the purity of essence that give us the ability to achieve our own perfection in whatever we do.

## State of Exhaustion

> The perfection of mental silence is only to settle scattered and confused awareness.
>
> ZEN MASTER DAHUI[2]

In New York, many of the parents and children that I met seemed to be in a constant state of exhaustion as they rushed around to sports matches, music practices and extra tuition classes of all varieties. What seemed to be missing was the ability of many parents to spend time just communicating with their children. Nor, despite an obsessive interest in child-rearing practices, did many of the children appear to be encouraged to enjoy the special aspect of childhood: the ability to be in the present moment – lost in the magic of their own imagination. The 'flow state' appears to be a natural ability that children have in their creative play but it is soon blurred by the influences of the socializing process involved in growing older; it needs to be appreciated and developed. Whether in the child or the creative adult, this appears to be the state in which we are most fulfilled. An increased sense of self-esteem and contentment seem to be by-products we gain when we are achieving our best performance in whatever we do. For many children in today's chaotic world, where minds are scattered and coloured with emotional problems, there is a constant round of underachievement and disappointment. Eventually labelled 'difficult children', many young people end up on the way to becoming disturbed adults.

Many of the children with whom I worked in New York came from backgrounds filled with problems. Far from being disinterested in the meditation programme, however, they were full of enthusiasm and seemed to have little trouble relating these concepts to all aspects of their own lives. This was despite the fact that this programme concentrates on a spiritual approach to life, and on long-term gains, rather than on instant results.

## Self-focusing

For most people, even those with no real problems, it is very difficult to remain focused. It is even more difficult when we are approaching an anxiety-provoking situation such as an exam, a competition or a concert. If we can train our minds to rise above self-focusing – to transcend our petty needs – then we can cope with all the pressures of performance when the occasion arises.

If we train our minds by the use of Zen, we find that we have achieved a training for our entire lives, not just for a short time. We begin to live with true 'mindfulness', continually alert and aware, tuned into every action but clinging onto nothing – images and thoughts coming and going as if reflected in a mirror, leaving no traces after they have gone. By living this way, we can experience true joy as we live each day fully. As Vietnamese Zen Master, Thich Nhat Hanh, tells us:

> Self-confidence is re-established, the shadows of illusion no longer overwhelm us, and our concentration develops to its fullest.[3]

## Our Form of Zen

When I was being interviewed on the Sean Rafferty Radio show in Belfast a few years ago, a listener from Armagh rang in and made an interesting point. The caller explained that she had known an old man who always said: 'The man who doesn't live fully, doesn't live at all.' She finished by saying: '... that is our form of Zen'. This saying shows us the similarity between all forms of wisdom, great religions, philosophies and old folklore. The Christian and Jewish mystics, the Sufis, the Native Americans – all have their own form of Chinese Taoism, of Japanese Zen. Ultimately, peace and perfection can be found, not in a faraway country, but in the quiet of our own soul.

Successful living is all about living fully and enjoying life's journey. It is not necessarily about reaching a goal. The journey may often be a struggle but it is this daily journey that is the substance of life. The triumph of achievement of our goals is often momentary. Life is so fleeting that if we are only living for moments of glory we are not really living. Successful living is not about being the very best and getting to the top at whatever cost – it is about reaching into our 'centre of stillness', and becoming the best we can be.

## Easy Answers

Most of us are looking for easy answers – quick fixes which will provide us with an easy lifestyle and meet the needs of ourselves and our children. We seem to be demanding instant happiness not realising that the more we search and push for this intangible commodity, the less we find it. There really are, as – deep down – we all suspect, no quick solutions, no instant answers. We all see the outward rewards, the medals, the prizes, but what we do not see are the years of disciplined practice, of heartbreak, and of persistence that have preceded every success. True success is built on strong lasting foundations and is often not so visible. It is rarely found in the glamorous lives seen in newspapers but, rather, it can be found in the lives of people who cope, on a daily basis, with doing the best they can under life's difficult circumstances.

Several months after our return to Dublin from New York, I had a talk with Father Halley, the then President of Blackrock College, one of Dublin's more prominent secondary schools. He summed up the ideals of the school in a simple but effective way when he said: 'Here the boys are expected to do their very best and to avail of all the opportunities open to them.' Maybe if we could give a child a motto for life this should be it. Father Halley realised that all the boys under his care have different talents and interests, but if they can fulfil their true potential – whatever that may be – then they will have achieved excellence.

## Each Stage is a New Beginning

I feel that our lives are full of stages. These may be the usual transition stages, such as adolescence and middle age, but age may not even be a factor. The important stages may be periods of years when we experience times of crisis or change. These times may be seen with apprehension or as unpredictable periods of change or disorder. On the other hand, each stage may be viewed as a new beginning – as an exciting period of challenge and growth. Once again, it is our perception of the events rather than the events themselves that matters.

Each time that I move to a different country I start a new chapter in my life, learning new things and developing my existing ideas further. This is not without pain and difficulty, as everyone who has moved country knows. However, I try to tell myself: 'This is a new beginning, not a disruptive upheaval.' On some occasions, I'm more successful at this than on others. I know, however, that if I take this attitude everything will work out far more positively. It may not, however, work out the way I expected or, indeed, the way I thought I wanted it to turn out; so I find I have to let go of my preconceptions and realise there is a time for everything.

## Wisdom of the Native American Culture

In New York, I was able to develop my interest in education and creativity and learn something about the culture of the

Native Americans. This was a culture about which I had previously known very little. In Bronxville, New York, there is a small plaque on a stone wall near the railway station which reads:

Sunset Hill
Where in the year 1666
Gramattan,
Chief of the Mohican Indians
Signed the Deed transferring
Eastchester to the White Man

Bronxville, a commuters' suburb thirty minutes from Grand Central Station, now bears little trace of past Native American culture. Perfect lawns have the neat appearance of being manicured daily and the pretty main street resembles a small English village. It was here, however, that social studies teacher Tim Chapman helped me to open my eyes, and those of my children, to the beauty and wisdom of the Native American culture. Tim has great knowledge of this culture and tremendous respect for it and he was always able to impart these gifts to his classes.

My husband, children and I travelled across the United States learning more about Native American culture as we went, all the while searching out similarities between the ancient traditions of the world. In New Mexico, we went to the Pueblo village of Taos where the famous psychoanalyst, Carl Jung, had held discussions, many years previously, in which he had compared his views with those of the Native American Chiefs. The depth and wisdom of the Native American culture also reflects the words of a Chinese tenth-century Zen master, who tells us:

A brief time of silence, a moment of stillness gradually build up into correct concentration.

YUNG-MING[4]

## Breaking down Barriers

Over the last decade, my work with both schoolchildren and adults, who were involved in various artistic activities, has been very exciting as, together, we have taken great strides forward – breaking down barriers and producing innovative results.

It was particularly wonderful for me – and the teachers with whom I worked – to see young children attaining the high level of good results that they achieved. Many of the children that I met in New York came from socially disadvantaged backgrounds where intellectual stimulation often plays a very minor part. The test scores and attitudes of these children have shown that they too can respond very well to creative teaching and stimulating ideas. These children, even more than those from privileged backgrounds, need to be shown the relevance of what they are doing – how what they learn today will be meaningful for the future. Mary Spellman is still working on these ideas at Public School 97, in the Bronx, and the children there are still eagerly asking for the 'Breathing Techniques'.

The concept of the 'zone' and the connection with it to meditation or breathing techniques are very difficult ideas to explain verbally. It was, therefore, fascinating to see that small children appeared to readily understand the significance of these ideas just as easily as do college students and older individuals.

## Amazing Improvements

> Mindfulness is the miracle by which we master and restore ourselves.
>
> THICH NHAT HAHN[5]

Although no rigorous scientific study was undertaken, some of the improvements in the children's test scores were amazing and both children and teachers were very pleased with these results. One particularly interesting factor was the way the children adapted the meditation to fit their own lifestyle. In the areas of music, art and dance the results were equally exciting for young children and older individuals. Creative professionals and children have all been able to tune into the vital centre, the source of creativity. As we gently breathe, we touch this centre of perfection which we might also call 'God' or 'Ultimate Reality', depending on our cultural background and philosophical views. Our minds can be emptied of thoughts and distractions. This is not the nihilistic emptiness of the West but '... a universe of the spirit in which everything communicates freely with everything, transcending bounds, limitless'.[6]

This state is one of personal perfection – not necessarily the perfection of world standards. This is no guarantee that we can become a top artist or musician, but we can become the best within the confines of our own talent – that surely is success.

## Creative Lives

> Always keep your mind as bright and clear as the vast sky, the great ocean, and the highest peak, empty of all thought.
>
> MORIHEI UESHIBA[7]

Whether in a primary school in the middle of the Bronx, New York, or in a stately boys' college overlooking Dublin Bay, the aim of educators is the same – to set out to help individuals to achieve their full potential so that they can go on to live constructive, creative lives. On these aims we base our hopes for a strong, caring, productive society of the twenty-first century. In order to achieve this, maybe it is now time to teach students, of all ages, the art of meditation. We can help them – and ourselves – to feel more in control and to harness the necessary energy to achieve an all-round optimal performance.

As Dag Hammarskjöld realised, many years ago, when he set up the meditation room in the United Nations building in New York, we should all learn to transcend 'the self' and reach into the silent depths of our 'centre of stillness'. Hammarskjöld had an ideal of peace in a world that had gone terribly wrong. It was an ideal that would need to start with children so that the world might never lose the integrity and wonder of youth.

---

When I was doing the test I was using the breathing and it helped me much better to Concentrate and I really thought the test was easy and when I got nervous I was Concentrating on the feather. The questions were easy when I was concentrationing. I hope I did my best that I could do.

---

# NOTES

**Chapter 1**

1. Hammarskjöld, Dag, *Markings*, London: Faber, 1991.
2. Franck, Frederick, *Zen Seeing, Zen Drawing*, New York: Bantam Books, 1993.
3. Ueshiba, Morihei; Stevens, John (trans.), *The Art of Peace*, Boston and London: Shambhala, 1997.
4. Hass, Robert (ed.), *The Essential Haiku, Versions of Basho, Buson, and Issa*, New Jersey: The Ecco Press, 1994.
5. Heathcote, Felicity, *Peak Performance: Zen and the Sporting Zone*, Dublin: Wolfhound Press, 1996.
6. Waley, Arthur, *The Way and its Power*, London: Unwin Paperbacks, 1977.
7. Heathcote, Felicity, *Peak Performance: Zen and the Sporting Zone*, Dublin: Wolfhound Press, 1996.
8. Suzuki, Daisetz T., *Zen and Japanese Culture*, New York: MJF Books, 1959.
9. Borgenicht, David (ed.), *Native American Wisdom*, Philadelphia and London: Running Press, 1994.
10. Cleary, Thomas (trans.), *Zen Lessons: The Art of Leadership*, Boston and London: Shambhala, 1987.

**Chapter 2**

1. Herrigel, Eugen, *Zen in the Art of Archery*, London: Arkana, 1985.
2. Cleary, Thomas, *The Five Houses of Zen*, Boston and London: Shambhala, 1997.
3. Ming-Dao, Deng, *365 Tao Daily Meditations*, San Francisco: Harper, 1992.
4. Goleman, Daniel, *Emotional Intelligence*, London: Bloomsbury Paperbacks, 1996.

5. Cleary, Thomas, *The Five Houses of Zen*, Boston and London: Shambhala, 1997.
6. Ueshiba, Morihei; Stevens, John (trans.), *The Art of Peace*, Boston and London: Shambhala, 1997.

**Chapter 3**

1. Arden, Harvey and Wall, Steve, *Wisdom Keepers*, Hillsboro, OR: Beyond Words Publishing, 1990.
2. Cleary, Thomas (trans.), *Zen Lessons: The Art of Leadership*, Boston and London: Shambhala, 1987.
3. Emerson, Ralph Waldo; Turner, Peter (ed.), *Nature and Other Writings*, Boston and London: Shambhala, 1994.
4. Cleary, Thomas (trans. and ed.), *Zen Essence: The Science of Freedom*, Boston and London: Shambhala, 1995.
5. Morgan, Genevieve (ed.), *Monet the Artist Speaks*, San Francisco: Collins.
6. Heathcote, Felicity, *Peak Performance: Zen and the Sporting Zone*, Dublin: Wolfhound Press, 1996.
7. Herrigel, Eugen, *The Method of Zen*, London: Arkana, 1988.
8. Saito, Ryukyu, *Japanese Ink-Painting: Lessons in Suiboku Technique*, Rutland, Vermont and Tokyo: Charles E. Tuttle Co., 1991.
9. Izutsu, Toshihiko, *Towards a Philosophy of Zen Buddhism*, Tehran: Imperial Iranian Academy of Philosophy, 1977,
10. Nicholson, Reynold A. (trans.), *Rūmī, Poet and Mystic 1207–1273*, London: George Allen and Unwin Ltd, 1950.
11. Deshimaru, Taisen, *Questions to a Zen Master*, New York: Arkana, 1985.
12. Lisle, Laurie, *Portrait of an Artist: A Biography of Georgia O'Keeffe*, New York: Washington Square Press, Simon & Schuster Inc., 1981.
13. Curtis, Natalie (ed.), *The Indians' Book: Songs and Legends of the American Indian*, New York: 1907.
14. De Mello, Anthony, *The Way to Love: The Last Meditations of Anthony De Mello*, New York: Image Books, Doubleday, 1995.
15. *Collected Poems and Plays of Rabindranath Tagore*, Macmillan, 1977.

**Chapter 4**

1. Arberry, A.J., *Hafiz: Fifty Poems*, Cambridge: Cambridge University Press, 1974.
2. Stevens, John (trans.), *Dewdrops on a Lotus Leaf, Zen poems of Ryokan*, Shambhala, Centaur Editions, 1993.
3. Ibid.
4. Hass, Robert (ed.), *The Essential Haiku, Versions of Basho, Buson, and Issa*, New Jersey: The Ecco Press, 1994.

5. *The Genius of Haiku, Readings from R.H. Blyth*, Tokyo: The Hokuseido Press, 1995.
6. Ibid.
7. Bradbury, Ray, *Zen in the Art of Writing*, Bantam Books, 1992.
8. Franck, Frederick, *Zen Seeing, Zen Drawing*, New York: Bantam Books, 1993.
9. Bode, Carl (ed.), *The Portable Thoreau*, New York: Viking Penguin Books, 1982.
10. Ibid.
11. Dawson, Carl, *Lafcadio Hearn and the Vision of Japan*, The Johns Hopkins University Press, 1992.
12. Frankl, Victor, *Man's Search for Meaning*, New York: Simon and Schuster, 1984.
13. *The Whole Shebang, McDonald's Young Writers*, Dublin: The O'Brien Press, 1998.
14. Ming-Dao, Deng, *365 Tao Daily Meditations*, San Francisco: Harper, 1992.


**Chapter 5**


1. Leggett, Trevor, *Zen and the Ways*, Rutland, Vermont and Tokyo: Charles E. Tuttle Co., 1987.
2. *Samadhi, The State of Total Unstrained Concentration or Absorption.*
3. *The Mysticism Of Sound And Music, The Sufi Teaching of Hazrat Inayat Khan*, Boston and London: Shambhala, Dragon Editions, 1996.
4. Csikszentmihalyi, Mihaly, *The Evolving Self*, HarperCollins, 1993.
5. Herrigel, Eugen, *Zen in the Art of Archery*, London: Arkana, 1985.
6. *The Mysticism of Sound and Music, The Sufi Teaching of Hazrat Inayat Khan*, Boston and London: Shambhala, Dragon Editions, 1996.
7. Jackson, Phil and Delehanty, Hugh, *Sacred Hopes*, New York: Hyperion, 1995.
8. Heathcote, Felicity, *Peak Performance: Zen and the Sporting Zone*, Dublin: Wolfhound Press, 1996.
9. Johnson, Spencer, *The Precious Present*, Hertfordshire: Exley Publications, 1998.
10. Deshimaru, Taisen, *Questions to a Zen Master*, New York: Arkana, 1985.


**Chapter 6**


1. Hahn, Thich Nhat, *Zen Keys*, New York: Image Books, Doubleday, 1995.
2. Deshimaru, Taisen, *The Zen Way to the Martial Arts*, New York: Arkana, 1991.
3. Hirai, Tomio, *Zen and the Mind (Scientific Approach to Zen Practice)*, Tokyo: Japan Publications Inc., 1978.

4. Hahn, Thich Nhat, *The Miracle of Mindfulness*, London: Rider Books, 1991.
5. Hirai, Tomio, *Zen Meditation Therapy*, Tokyo: Japan Publications Inc., 1975.
6. Sekida, Katsuki, *Zen Training*, Weatherhill, 1975.
7. Ohiyesa; Eastman, Dr Charles A. (trans.), *The Soul of the Indian, an Interpretation*, Boston: McClure, Phillips, 1902.

**Chapter 7**

1. Rabindranath, Tagore, *Collected Poems and Plays*, Macmillan, 1977.
2. Cleary, Thomas (trans.), *The Art of War by Sun Tzu*, Boston and London: Shambhala, Dragon Editions, 1988.
3. Lasalle, Enomiya H.M., *Zen Meditations for Christians*, Illinois: Open Court, 1974.
4. Fitzgerald, Edward (trans.), *Rubáiyát of Omar Khayyám*, Hertfordshire: Wordsworth Editions Limited, 1993.

**Chapter 8**

1. Cleary, Thomas (trans. and ed.), *Zen Essence: The Science of Freedom*, Boston and London: Shambhala, 1995.
2. Ibid.
3. Hanh, Thich Nhat. *Zen Keys*, New York: Image Books, Doubleday, 1995.
4. Cleary, Thomas, *The Five Houses of Zen*, Boston and London: Shambhala, 1997.
5. Hahn, Thich Nhat, *The Miracle of Mindfulness*, London: Rider Books, 1991.
6. Kawabata, Yasunari; Seidensticker, E.G. (trans.), *Japan the Beautiful and Myself*, Tokyo: Kodansha International Ltd, 1974.
7. Ueshiba, Morihei; Stevens, John (trans.), *The Art of Peace*, Boston and London: Shambhala, 1997.